Perspectives in Linguistics

Perspectives in Linguistics

JOHN T. WATERMAN

Phoenix Books

THE UNIVERSITY OF CHICAGO PRESS

This book is also available in a clothbound edition from
THE UNIVERSITY OF CHICAGO PRESS

Library of Congress Catalog Card Number: 63-9732

THE UNIVERSITY OF CHICAGO PRESS, CHICAGO & LONDON
The University of Toronto Press, Toronto 5, Canada

To My Wife

PREFACE

Scientiae enim per additamenta fiunt, non enim est possibile eundem incipere et finire.

—GUY DE CHAULIAC

If the student of linguistics or the structural grammarian is to become something more than a well-trained technician, he must sooner or later develop an awareness of his intellectual heritage; he must learn that the ideas which he finds so new and so stimulating are rooted in a long tradition. This is a necessary but frequently neglected part of his education.

As this book goes to press there is no readily available text that adequately provides this perspective. To my knowledge, only one of the recent linguistics texts published in this country does more than mention in passing the names of those scholars—other than Bloomfield—who first formulated and clarified the principles of structuralism. And because linguistics has come to mean so exclusively "structural linguistics," the origins and the theoretical basis of comparative linguistics are often treated most cursorily. The fact that the one would have been impossible without the other is scarcely suggested.

Although I deal at some length with the development of structuralism in linguistics, I do not discuss specific methodologies of what I call—for want of a better term—"American structuralism." This is the one perspective which the reader of a book such as this probably already has or at least to which he has easy access, either in a course of instruction or through one of the several excellent texts that are available. I have tried instead to place major emphasis upon those perspectives which are more likely not only to be lacking, but which might even be somewhat difficult to acquire without special orientation and guidance.

Although this book contains little that is new, I trust that some

of the things I have to say about Jacob Grimm, as well as my
efforts to relate his accomplishments to the work and progress of
later scholars, will be accepted as a valid interpretation. To the extent that my comments do honor to the name of this gifted, learned,
and dedicated scholar, may they stand as a very minor tribute to
his memory, as we prepare to observe the centennial anniversary
of his death.

J. T. W

Los Angeles, 1962

CONTENTS

The Study of Language in Ancient Times 1

Medieval and Early Modern Periods 11

The Nineteenth Century 18

The Twentieth Century to 1950 61

Table of Phonetic Symbols 99

Bibliography 101

Index 103

ix

THE STUDY OF LANGUAGE
IN ANCIENT TIMES

The most ancient expressions of linguistic interest generally known to the Western world are recorded in the second and eleventh chapters of the Book of Genesis in the Old Testament. The first reference is to the naming of the animals (Gen. 2:19–20):

> And out of the ground the Lord God formed every beast of the field, and every fowl of the air; and brought them unto Adam to see what he would call them: and whatsoever Adam called every living creature, that was the name thereof. And Adam gave names to all cattle, and to the fowl of the air, and to every beast of the field. . . .

In chapter 11 of Genesis, verses 1–19, is recorded the account of the Tower of Babel:

> And the whole earth was of one language, and of one speech. And it came to pass, as they journeyed from the east, that they found a plain in the land of Shinar; and they dwelt there. And they said one to another, Go to, let us make brick, and burn them throughly. And they had brick for stone, and slime had they for morter. And they said, Go to, let us build us a city and a tower, whose top may reach unto heaven; and let us make us a name, lest we be scattered abroad upon the face of the whole earth. And the Lord came down to see the city and the tower, which the children of men builded. And the Lord said, Behold, the people is one, and they have all one language; and this they begin to do: and now nothing will be restrained from them, which they have imagined to do. Go to, let us go down, and there confound their language, that they may not understand one another's speech. So the Lord scattered them abroad from thence upon the face of

1

all the earth: and they left off to build the city. Therefore is the name of it called Babel; because the Lord did there confound the language of all the earth: and from thence did the Lord scatter them abroad upon the face of all the earth.

Most civilizations and cultures—in their sacred writings, in their oral traditions, in their folklore—have some reference to the origin and occasionally to the dispersion of speech. Only rarely (at least in the records that have come down to us) did the ancients try to learn something about speech phenomena by observation or experimentation. The Greek historian Herodotos (fifth century B.C.) records one such incident: an Egyptian king named Psammetichos wished to determine which of the world's languages was oldest. To gain this information he decided to isolate two newborn infants until such time as they should begin to speak; the assumption being that, lacking any pattern to imitate, they would therefore instinctively employ the most primitive of natural languages. In the course of time the children were heard to utter something that was recorded as *bekos*—which turned out to be phonetically similar to the Phrygian word for "bread." Therefore, Phrygian (once spoken in Asia Minor) was held to be the first language of mankind, at least by King Psammetichos and—we may presume—by his court.

Linguistic investigation in the conventional sense of the word, however, could not begin until philosophy and the analytic study of language had been developed. And this goal was not realized until the Greeks and the Indians applied their peculiar genius toward investigating the nature of language. Although they had certain goals in common—such as the clarification of the already obsolescent idiom of the Homeric poems and of the Vedic hymns—their respective approaches to the study of language were fundamentally different. By and large the Greeks speculated about language, whereas the Indians described it.

The earliest Indian literature is religious in theme, consisting of ritualistic hymns composed in a language called Vedic Sanskrit, to distinguish it from the later Classical Sanskrit. Although not recorded until approximately 800 B.C., the language of the oldest of these hymns is held to be considerably older. With the passage of time this ancient form of Indic, as well as the somewhat later variety known as Classical Sanskrit or simply Sanskrit (the borderline between Vedic and Classical Sanskrit is not sharply drawn), became less and less accessible; a situation that posed special problems for the Hindu priests and scholars, since they believed that the efficacy of certain religious ceremonies depended not only upon the faithfulness of the received text to the original language of the hymns, but also upon an oral rendition accurately reflecting the original pronunciation. Although educational practices coupled with religious zeal had preserved and handed down a most detailed corpus of grammatical and phonetic information, a knowledge of the older language would in time surely have perished, had it not eventually been written down.

This feat was accomplished by the most famous of Indian grammarians, Pāṇini, writing toward the end of the fourth century B.C. His grammar, the first of which we have any knowledge, remains to this day the most marvelously succinct and definitive statement of Sanskrit ever written. It is not a grammar in the conventional sense of the term—indeed, one must be an accomplished Sanskritist even to "read" it!—but rather an algebra-like condensation of the structure of the language, consisting of some four thousand *Sūtras* ("strings") or aphorisms. Obviously, one "reads" Pāṇini's grammar in about the same way we "read" the Periodic Table or the structural formulas of chemistry. In both cases we need a great deal of background. As a matter of fact—with respect to Pāṇini's work —Indian linguistics is little more than one grand, protracted effort to elucidate and elaborate his grammar, an effort culminating in the *Great Commentary* (*Mahābhāṣya*) of Patañjali (second half of second century B.C.). Later treatises are essentially "commentaries on the commentaries."

The Sanskrit word for grammar is *Vyākaraṇa*, which means "separation, analysis." True to this sense, Indian grammar is almost wholly analytic and descriptive. As pointed out earlier, the practical goal of linguistic study was to establish the morphology and phonology of an archaic and obsolescent language. In this the Indian grammarians were singularly successful, due in part to their objective approach, but no doubt due also to the structure of the language itself, for it is an idiom in which the affixing of grammatical elements to a root, and the joining together of simple words to form compounds, is beautifully formalized and obvious. Not so obvious at first blush, of course, since one must first learn how to resolve the phonetic "mergings" that have taken place between roots, affixes, and even larger phrasal elements, for written Sanskrit is roughly analogous to a phonetic transcription. It reflects quite accurately the desired pronunciation, and leaves to the reader the task of resolving the phonetic combinations into discrete lexical units—much as if we were to write something like *Jeetawredi?* and rely upon the reader to convert this into "Did you eat already?" However, once the external and internal phonetic combinations (called *sandhi*) have been accounted for, the neat structure of the language becomes apparent. At this stage of analysis, the student works his way back from some larger grammatical unit to a root, listing and identifying each element that has been affixed in some manner to the root: somewhat analogous to taking a word like *ungentlemanly* and breaking it down into *un-gentle-man-ly*, accompanying each step in the analysis with a statement as to the function and meaning of the unit under discussion. A Sanskrit dictionary, incidentally, consists principally of roots, not "words" as we normally use the term.

The Indian grammarians scarcely mention what we customarily refer to as "syntax"—the grammar of the sentence. Of course, one can argue that the borderline between "phrase" and "sentence" is at best tenuous; however, it is equally true that the linking together of phrases in Sanskrit is not nearly so complicated a procedure as, say, in Latin or Greek.

Although they frequently tried their hand at etymologies, the Indians accomplished little of enduring value in this area. Much of their prose is given over to interpretations of their poetic works, in a manner reminiscent of our Bible commentaries, and although a detailed word-study is characteristic of this sort of exegesis, the results are sometimes fanciful and scientifically unreliable.

It is interesting to speculate about what direction Western grammar might have taken had it derived from the carefully descriptive studies of the Indians rather than from the speculative flights of Greek philosophy. Be that as it may, it was the Greeks, in grammar as in so many other things, who gave to the Western world an approach to the analysis of language that has endured almost unchanged even unto the present day—for better or for worse.

The earliest extant document in Greek dealing with the subject of language is one of Plato's (425–348/47 B.C.) dialogues, the *Cratylus*. Not only is this the earliest recorded instance of Greek linguistic expression; it is also one of the most important, for in it is presented the philosophical doctrine that language arose "by nature" (*physis:* "nature, inborn quality"). Although the meaning of the text is sometimes quite obscure, Plato apparently believed that there was an ontologically valid and compelling connection between a thing and its name, for he taught (or, more accurately, he accepted and developed the doctrine) that the only enduring reality is an intellectual reality existing essentially in the world of ideas. "Things" are but lower-level physical extensions or counterparts of these idealistic prototypes. Language, therefore—and by "language" Plato means "vocabulary"—probably arose by *necessity:* words *had* to have a certain predetermined meaning, because they could only reflect the immutable and eternal nature of the Idea. A corollary of this doctrine, of course, is that language can only be logical and reasonable, even though in practice we may not always be able to establish the relationship between the shadowy things of the sense world and the intelligible realities of Ideas.

As erudite as his philosophy may sound, Plato's attempt to clarify it by examples—as he does in the *Cratylus*—results in some incredibly naïve etymologizing. In fact, some scholars cannot be-

lieve that he was serious; they feel he must have been joking. However, professional philosophers are not noted for their published
humor, and I rather suspect that Plato meant most of what he
wrote about the history and meaning of words.

As an example of his method, at one place in the dialogue he has
Socrates explaining to his young friends Hermogenes and Cratylus
why the Greek word for "air" is *aēr*. He quotes a verbal form, *airei*,
which may be translated "it raises," and, after noting its phonetic
similarity to the word *aēr*, concludes that "air" is so called because
it is capable of "raising" things like leaves and smoke from the
ground. In this case, however, he is not absolutely sure of his
etymology, since he quotes another possibility, the phrase *aei
rhei*, "always flows," which might also he thinks be the philosophical justification for the term *aēr*. Unfortunately, modern
etymologists can demonstrate quite conclusively that the phonetic
similarities between *aēr*, *airei*, and *aei rhei* are entirely fortuitous,
and that none of the words is related to any of the others.

Plato's most distinguished pupil, Aristotle (384–322/21 B.C.), differed with his master as to the origin and nature of language. Aristotle, the father of grammar in the Occidental world, believed and
taught (see his essay entitled *On Interpretation*) that language was
arrived at by *convention* or *agreement*. To describe this process he
uses the Greek words *thesis* and *synthēkē*, meaning "arrangement"
and "convention," respectively. He opposed what he considered to
be the Platonic doctrine that real being belongs only to the Ideas or
Universals, whose existence is independent of the objects that imperfectly manifest them. Aristotle believed that every object in the
world is a union of two ultimate principles: matter and form (or
essence), the latter force yielding the potential or power to determine the structure of matter. In things linguistic, therefore, he did
not feel compelled to search for the rationale behind every name or
utterance, since to him the fact that language presented to the
observer something formed and structured was, in itself, philosophical proof of its reality. The particular form that a given word
assumed was merely one of an infinite number of possible material
embodiments. He did not, therefore, do much etymologizing, since

the problem of "original meaning" was of little importance to him. At some time or another a word had come into being because two or more people had agreed to symbolize a certain thing by reference to a given linguistic configuration. Whatever reasons may have entered into this process of selection, they were quite arbitrary; any of a dozen reasons might have served equally well.

This is the view adopted by most linguists today. Language is arbitrary. A Spaniard says *caballo* because his ancestors at one time said *caballus*, not because there is anything about the term *caballo* (or *caballus*) that suggests a four-legged domesticated animal known to speakers of English as a horse. This viewpoint does not, by the way, disclaim the validity of sound-symbolism: onomato-poetic derivation. Linguists do not deny the obvious force of onomatopoeia in language formation; what *is* denied is that there is any *necessity* attached to this naming. Otherwise, of course, all languages would use the same imitative words—which they certainly do not.

From its very beginnings Greek linguistics was closely aligned with philosophy. The notions of language origins held by both Plato and Aristotle were predicated upon philosophical doctrines concerning the nature of reality and knowledge, and in no important sense were they derived from an inspection of linguistic data; although Aristotle, in addition to his philosophical speculating, did make some empirically based observations about the Greek language. He investigated the parts of speech, for instance, distinguishing nouns, verbs, and a third catch-all class he called "conjunctions."

True to its origins, the study of language among the Greeks remained the special province of the philosophers, and all the important "schools" contributed something. The Stoics (founded 308 B.C. in Athens by Zeno), for example, formulated much of our traditional grammar. Continuing the study of case-relationships begun by Aristotle, they devised the names of the cases that have come down to us in Latin translation.

The very word "case" derives via French from the Latin *casus*, itself a translation of Greek *ptōsis*, meaning "fall." The Stoics held

that all the cases had "fallen away" from the original case, the
nominative—the case of the *nomen* or "name." Unfortunately, the
Greek terminology did not always fare so well in translation. The
accusative case, as an example, was called by the Greeks *aitiatikē*,
that is, "the thing caused by the verb." But *aitia* means both
"cause" and "accusation," and certain of the Latin grammarians
later called it the "accusing" case rather than the "causing." Today we should really refer to the "causative case," but tradition
has frozen the mistranslation into our terminology, and it will
probably stay there forever.

In many ways the Alexandrian Age of literature (roughly 300–
150 B.C.) may be considered the high point of Greek linguistic
studies. This was the age of Aristarchus, especially noted for his
analysis of the language of the Homeric poems; of Apollonios
Dyskolos, writer on syntax and student of the literary dialects of
Greek; Dionysios Thrax, who wrote the first formal grammar of
Greek: a book of less than four hundred lines, yet acknowledged to
be the prototype for all subsequent conventional grammars of both
Greek and Latin.

Oddly enough, the Greeks, whose intellectual curiosity was well-
nigh insatiable, showed almost no interest in any language other
than their own. This fact is all the more remarkable when we remember that the armies of Alexander the Great roamed the then-
known world as far to the east as India, and from the shores of the
seas called Black and Caspian in the north to the waters of the
Persian Gulf and the Arabian Sea in the south. And yet not a word
about the speech of the peoples occupying those vast stretches! The
ships of all nations dropped anchor in Hellas' ports-of-call, and
Greek merchants sold their wares in Egypt, Babylonia, and Italy,
conversing much of the time no doubt in the local tongues. But, of
course, the foreigners were all barbarians—all "babblers"—and,
too, the gods on Mount Olympus spoke Greek. Only one language
other than their own ever merited even passing consideration: We
know of two works—since vanished—that dealt with Latin; and
one of these had as its theme the proposition that Latin was derived
from Greek. Centuries later, to be sure (fifth century A.D.), Hesych-

ios compiled a dictionary in which he listed words not only from Greek and Latin, but also from many other languages, most of them located in Asia and Asia Minor. This lexicon is especially treasured because of its multilingual word-lists, and also because certain of these languages are otherwise most skimpily preserved. But a dictionary tells us very little about the structure of a language. And—this is true certainly of Hesychios' lexicon—we have few hints as to pronunciation, a drawback attending most older dictionaries. The Greeks, incidentally, tell us next to nothing about how their language was pronounced.

In summary, the Greeks approached language by way of metaphysics, bequeathing to the world a form of linguistic analysis which has come to be known as "philosophical grammar." The term is used here without reproach, for theirs was an intellectual achievement of awesome proportions. Not only did they succeed in describing in a highly satisfactory manner their own intricate language, but they gave to posterity an intellectual discipline and a tool that may still one day be reckoned superior to certain of our twentieth-century linguistic "-isms."

As in so many other areas of learning and culture, the Romans were content to accept the legacy of Greece. Their dictionaries and grammars are all cast in traditional Grecian mold.

The first Latin grammar of consequence was compiled by Varro (116–27 B.C.), and bears the straightforward title *De lingua Latina*. Consisting originally of twenty-six books, only numbers five through ten have come down to us. Mention should also be made of Quintilian's (*ca.* A.D. 35–90) *Institutio oratoria*, although, as the title indicates, it is devoted mainly to rhetoric. Aside from these, about the only other grammatical work of enduring significance is the *Ars minor* of Aelius Donatus, who taught in Rome around the middle of the fourth century A.D. His grammar was widely used for elementary instruction well into the Middle Ages. As evidence of its influence and popularity, it was the first book to be printed by means of wooden type.

With the slow disintegration and collapse of the empire during the fourth and fifth centuries, Rome could no longer maintain a climate conducive to intellectual pursuits, and many of her scholars and men of letters found refuge in the new capital on the Bosporus, Constantinople. It was here that Priscian (512–60) wrote his elaborate *Grammatical Categories*, the standard Latin grammar of the Middle Ages, consisting of eighteen books devoted to the parts of speech (*Priscianus maior*) and two books to syntax (*Priscianus minor*).

Likewise in the field of etymology the Romans did not get beyond their Greek models. The outstanding accomplishment in Latin is the etymological dictionary of St. Isidore of Seville (*ca.* 570–639), *Origines sive etymologiae*. But just as Plato in the *Cratylus*, so the Latin authors in their writings gave free rein to the imagination when searching for reasons *why* a word had a given meaning. The word *vulpēs* "fox," for example, was explained as being derived from *volō* "I fly" plus *pēs* "foot," thus meaning "fly-foot"; or *lepus* "hare" was supposedly compounded from *levis* "light" and *pēs* "foot." As is obvious from the examples, no proof of linguistic relationship or of regular phonetic correspondences valid throughout the language was required. The wildest guesses were not only admissible but entirely in order, even the notion that things could be named from opposing qualities. In line with this reverse logic, *bellum* "war" was explained as coming from the adjective *bellus* "beautiful" because war is *not* beautiful! Latin etymological works contain many such bizarre derivations.

Obviously, this survey touches only the most prominent and enduring monuments of linguistic activity among the Ancients—and certainly not even all of these, as a glance at one of the larger specialized handbooks will reveal. However, as far as grammatical theory and practice are concerned, the Western world followed faithfully the paths marked out by the Greeks. Although we must mention briefly certain achievements of the late Middle Ages and Early Modern period, we shall find little actually new in the study of language until we reach the eighteenth, or even indeed, the nineteenth century.

MEDIEVAL AND EARLY MODERN PERIODS

The spread of Christianity had as one of its secular benefits a vast widening of linguistic horizons. In accordance with Christ's commission to the Apostles to go into all the world and preach the Gospel to every creature, missionaries ventured far beyond the boundaries of the Greco-Roman world. Translating the Scriptures into the vernaculars became a principal task for Christian scholars, with the result that we can date many of the great Bible translations from these centuries: the Armenian (fifth century), the Gothic (fourth century), the Old Church Slavonic (ninth century). From these centuries, too, are dated many of the collections of words known as "glosses"—originally marginal translations or paraphrasings into some vernacular of Latin words and expressions intended to help the reader, presumably a priest, in his preaching and catechizing. Indeed, glossaries such as these occasionally constitute some of our oldest records of certain languages; German is such an instance.

Training the clergy involved, of course, the teaching of Latin, for which Priscian was the principal authority, although a textbook written in 1199 by Alexander de Villa Dei entitled *Doctrinale puerorum* became the standard school grammar of the Middle Ages. Above and beyond the practical goal of becoming literate, however, Latin grammar was studied in its relation to philosophy, constituting as it did one of the branches (along with logic and rhetoric) of the *trivium:* the basic curriculum established by the Scholastics.

Although a practical knowledge of diverse linguistic types gradually became available to medieval scholars, this information could not become generally accessible until the introduction of printing with movable type. It is the sixteenth century, therefore, that deserves to be called Early Modern in things linguistic, for not until then was anything like a comprehensive survey of language possible. Almost overnight there appeared a spate of grammars and dictionaries, most of them dealing with the vernaculars rather than

11

the classical languages. Since this was also the age of geographical discoveries, it is not surprising to find among these early linguistic treatises accounts of faraway tongues, usually limited, however, to word-lists and phrases. Some of these descriptions—meager though they be—are extremely valuable. Our sole direct knowledge of Gothic as it lived on in the Crimea, for example, is limited to a word-list compiled by a Flemish nobleman, Ogier Ghiselin van Busbecq, who, on a diplomatic mission to Constantinople in the years 1560–62, recorded and subsequently published a list of words and phrases, dictated presumably by a native speaker of the last living dialect of an East Germanic language.

From this era are also dated the early attempts to survey all the then-known languages, such as C. Gesner's *Mithridates* (Zurich, 1555) and Hieronymus Megiser's *Specimens of Forty Languages* (Frankfort, 1592). This sort of activity reached its zenith later on in the eighteenth century, culminating in such works as *A Comparative Vocabulary of the World's Languages* (1786–89) by the German traveler and natural scientist, P. S. Pallas, and a similar work dealing with more than eight hundred languages by the Spanish Jesuit, Lorenzo Hervás y Panduro in 1800–1805. The last and perhaps best known work of this kind is the *Mithridates* of Johann Christoph Adelung, which contains the Lord's Prayer in over five hundred languages and dialects. This monumental enterprise was published in four parts over the years 1806–17, after Adelung's death.

Of works dealing with the general nature of language, probably the most important is the famous "Port Royal Grammar" of 1660. The title itself achieves a certain grandeur: *Grammaire générale et raisonnée contenant les fondamens de l'art de parler, expliqués d'une manière claire et naturelle. Les raisons de ce qui est commun à toutes les langues et des principales différences qui s'y rencontrent; et plusieurs remarques nouvelles sur la langue françoise.* This was one of several more or less contemporary attempts to give "reasonable explanations" for the facts of language: philosophical grammar in the grand tradition.

Etymology was no better off than it had been under the Greeks and Romans. Scholars assumed as an article of faith that Hebrew had been man's first language, and most etymological studies monotonously attempt to skew the facts to fit the theory—even as did James IV of Scotland (1488–1513), who, like King Psammetichos, is said to have interned two children in order to discover which was mankind's first language. He is reported to have determined that the children "spak very guid Ebrew." In the same, even if somewhat more learned, spirit, is the work of the Frenchman E. Guichard, who in 1606 compiled an etymological dictionary of Hebrew, Chaldaic, Syriac, Greek, Latin, French, Italian, Spanish, German, Flemish, and English. He maintained that words could be traced from language to language by adding, subtracting, inverting, and transposing letters, "the which is not hard to believe when we consider that the Hebrews write from right to left, and the Greeks and others from left to right." Other scholars, more patriotically inclined, proposed their own language as the original one. Probably the most celebrated linguistic chauvinist is the Dutchman, Goropius Becanus (1518–72). A close runner-up, however, is the Swede, Andreas Kemke, who maintained that in the Garden of Eden God spoke Swedish, Adam Danish, and the serpent French.

The medieval and Early Modern eras—that is, until about the end of the eighteenth century—witnessed a tremendous increase in the *amount of information* about language. Significantly, however, the *methods of analysis and interpretation* were still those of the Ancients. A scientific approach had to wait until the nineteenth century, although of course there were those whom we may appropriately call precursors. Three of these—Gottfried Wilhelm von Leibniz, Johann Gottfried von Herder, and Sir William Jones—we shall now discuss.

Although Leibniz (1646–1716) is known to the world primarily as a philosopher and mathematician, he was in fact what the Germans call a *Universalgenie*, a scholar who commanded all the formal knowledge of his time. His background and interest in linguistics

were scarcely more than that of an extremely able and gifted dilet-
tante, yet he stands at the beginning of the modern era, pointing
the way toward a true science of language.

He was especially interested in studying the relationship of languages and establishing a linguistic genealogy. In order to achieve
anything substantial in these areas, Leibniz realized that scholars
would have to abandon their sterile practice of trying to relate all
languages to biblical Hebrew. Instead, he encouraged his contemporaries to examine and describe extant languages, and, on the
basis of mutually shared features, seek to establish valid genealo-
gies. He himself attempted just such a genealogy, although it must
be admitted that he, too, was not always guided by the facts. For
example, he suggests a very broad grouping of the "Eurasian" languages that derives more from intuition than from observation.
Nevertheless, he is the first known scholar to propose that all these
languages were derived from a common, prehistorical ancestor.
This thesis, in a modified form, has become the cardinal tenet of
comparative linguistics. Leibniz' classification of the languages of
Europe, Asia, and Egypt was printed in 1710 in the memoirs of the
Berlin Academy (*Miscellanea Berolinensia*).

Another area of concern to him was the collecting and describing
of living languages. As one of the leading intellectuals of his age,
Leibniz had a circle of acquaintances that was influential as well as
cosmopolitan. For instance, he persuaded the tsarina of Russia,
Catherine II, to subsidize P. S. Pallas' collection of specimens of
two hundred languages and dialects, and he urged the tsar, Peter
the Great, to have studies made of all the languages of the Russian
Empire, to have them reduced to writing, and to have dictionaries
and grammars prepared.

Leibniz, incidentally, was one of the earliest to champion the use
of the vernacular languages as vehicles of instruction and literature.
He was especially desirous that his fellow Germans take pride in
their tongue, study it, and cultivate it as a medium of polite and
learned discourse. In what must be considered a revolutionary

step for his time, he went so far as to publish several essays in German rather than in Latin or French, the only two academically acceptable languages of the day.

Johann Gottfried von Herder (1744–1803) is another eighteenth-century figure who did much to usher in the era of scientific linguistics. In 1772 he wrote a prize essay entitled *Concerning the Origin of Language (Über den Ursprung der Sprache)*. In this essay the German clergyman attacked the orthodox view of his age that speech is the direct gift of God. Herder rejected this belief, maintaining that language would be more logical if it were from God. Neither did he adopt the premise that man had invented language, but he held rather that the genesis of language was due to an impulse like that "of the mature embryo pressing to be born." Man, he concludes, is the only creature who has the ability to single out sensations: he alone is capable of conscious linguistic reflection. While accepting the belief that Hebrew was the original language, he believed that it developed of necessity from man's innermost nature. The speech-impulse itself, he concedes, is from God, but man has worked out his own linguistic destiny from that point on.

Not nearly so well known as Leibniz or Herder, but with more immediate and direct influence on nineteenth-century linguistics than either, was the Englishman, Sir William Jones (1746–94). Like the other two precursors we have discussed, Jones was not a professional philologist. Educated in the law, he served from 1783 until his death as a jurist on the bench of the British court of Calcutta in India. Throughout the last nine years of his brief life, Sir William studied Sanskrit, acquiring in the course of time not only a remarkable command of the language, but also—and of greater importance—a profound insight into its relationship to certain other languages. It is in fact customary to date the beginnings of modern comparative grammar in a general way from a statement contained in a speech which Jones delivered before the "Asiatick"

Society on February 2, 1786. Like so many momentous utterances, this one too is neither superficially spectacular nor obviously significant, and yet it is usually accepted as the first known printed statement of the fundamental postulate of comparative linguistics:

> The *Sanscrit* language, whatever be its antiquity, is of a wonderful structure; more perfect than the *Greek*, more copious than the *Latin*, and more exquisitely refined than either, yet bearing to both of them a stronger affinity, both in the roots of verbs and in the forms of grammar, than could possibly have been produced by accident; *so strong indeed, that no philologer could examine them all three, without believing them to have sprung from some common source, which, perhaps, no longer exists* [italics mine]: there is a similar reason, though not quite so forcible, for supposing that both the *Gothick* and the *Celtick*, though blended with a very different idiom, had the same origin with the *Sanscrit;* and the old *Persian* might be added to the same family.

Scholars before Jones had of course noticed the similarities between these various languages, but to the best of our knowledge no one prior to him had reached the conclusion—arrived at not by intuition but by inspection of the data—that these resemblances must be due to a common descent from a hypothetical earlier language "which, perhaps, no longer exists."

Once the authority of religion and tradition had been successfully challenged, the way was clear to approach the study of language in this new perspective. Scholars came to understand that language was in a state of constant flux, that it had a *history*, and that its genesis and development could be studied from the historical point of view. This—the notion of history applied to things other than wars and dynasties—was not generally appreciated until the late eighteenth and early nineteenth centuries. Applied to language it meant that scholars were now interested in tracing the records of speech as far back as possible, explaining language growth and change in the same manner as other historical phenomena, namely, by establishing a causal relationship between events bound together in time and space. From 1800 on, therefore, we may speak of the scientific study of language, or, to use the term in its narrower sense, "linguistics."

THE NINETEENTH CENTURY

The first systematic exposition of this new approach to linguistic research was made by a Dane, Rasmus Kristian Rask (1787–1832). In 1814 he submitted an essay to the Danish Academy of Science entitled *An Investigation into the Origin of the Old Norse or Icelandic Language* (*Undersøyelse om det Gamle Nordiske eller Islandske Sprogs Oprindelse*). The Danish Academy was conducting a contest, and the theme of the competition was: "To investigate and illustrate, with appropriate examples, by means of historical criticism, from what source the ancient Scandinavian language can most surely be derived; to state the character of the language and its relations, from ancient times and throughout the Middle Ages, to Scandinavian and Germanic dialects; and to determine exactly the fundamental principles upon which all derivations and comparisons in these languages should be built." That part of Rask's essay which deals with the last-mentioned objective is of paramount interest, because in developing this portion of his exposition he formulated certain basic principles and methods of modern comparative linguistics.

Rask emphasizes the necessity of methodically examining the total structure of a language; not merely selecting a few details or words and comparing them with similar phenomena in another tongue. He plays down the heavy emphasis which scholars were wont to place upon vocabulary agreement, pointing out that an almost limitless number of words passes back and forth between languages in geographical proximity, thus establishing an apparent sameness which in reality is due to borrowing and not to relationship. Of much greater importance is grammatical agreement because, no matter to what degree vocables are interchanged, languages rarely alter their structure in favor of outside influences. Failure to realize this, says Rask, robs most earlier investigations of their value. Although he stresses the importance of comparing

18

the morphology of languages, Rask perceived that phonetic agreement, provided some control over the method could be exercised, is another valuable means of determining linguistic relationship. His statement of this principle—upon which the modern comparative method is still based—deserves to be quoted:

> A language, however mixed it may be, belongs to the same branch of languages as another when it has the most essential, concrete, indispensable words, the foundation of the language, in common with it. . . . When agreement is found in such words in two languages, and so frequently that rules may be drawn up for the shift in letters [today we should say "sounds"] from one to the other, then there is a fundamental relationship between the two languages; especially when similarities in the inflectional system and in the general make-up of the languages correspond with them.

Rask's essay gives the clearest account of the aims and methods of comparative linguistics which was to be made for some years. Had he written in German or French rather than in Danish, and had the scope of his essay not been so limited, he might well have earned fame as the founder of modern linguistics. As it was, his essay won the prize and was printed in 1818. Its author, however, lived out a short, restless life and died, broken in health and fortune, at the age of forty-five. The honor he sought was bestowed—not unjustly nor undeservedly—upon a German professor whose name is familiar to millions as one of the editors and compilers of *Grimms' Fairy Tales*. Jacob Grimm wrote in German; he published a detailed comparative grammar of all the Germanic languages, and he elaborated upon Rask's largely correct but limited information. More important than all this, however, he perceived the phonetic principle underlying and binding together the phenomena that Rask had so astutely observed. Primarily for these reasons Grimm is held to be the father of comparative linguistics, but his debt to Rasmus Kristian Rask is enormous.

Jacob Grimm (1785–1863) was the first scholar to write a comparative grammar clearly dedicated to the new historico-organic method of research. In the Preface to the first volume of the first edition of his *German Grammar* ("German" here equals "Germanic"), Grimm emphasizes his wish to *describe* not *prescribe;* he is interested only in describing that which has grown naturally, and he advises every native-born German to forsake the pedantry of schoolmasters' rules and speak the language as he learned it at his mother's knee. In a revised Preface to a second edition of the first volume, he is even more specific in his insistence upon an unbiased approach to the facts of language: "I am hostile to notions of universal logic in grammar. They apparently lend themselves to exactness and solidarity of definition, but impede observation, which to me is the soul of linguistic science." Largely through the influence of Rask's essay—which he praises in the Preface to the first edition (1819) of his *Grammar*—Grimm came to realize the significance of phonology, that is, the study of the history of sounds within a given language or group of languages as preserved in written records. These were the *facts* of language. Grimm, like others of his era, did not distinguish carefully enough between letter and sound—his 595-page chapter on phonology bears the title: "Study of the Letters" (*Die Lehre von den Buchstaben*)—but even so, his comparison of the recorded versions of the various Germanic languages is reasonably rigorous. He was a child of his time and, as such, could not forego a certain amount of romantic speculation, as witnessed by his comments concerning certain sound changes that resulted in Old High German: ". . . from one point of view the sound shift seems to me to be a barbarous aberration from which other quieter nations refrained, but which has to do with the violent progress and yearning for liberty as found in Germany in the early Middle Ages, and which started the transformation of Europe."

Seen in proper perspective, however, both his methods of research and his findings were sound enough to insure his status as one of the greatest of the nineteenth-century linguists.

It should be made quite clear that Grimm was by no means the first who had been impressed by the obvious similarity between such languages as Greek and Latin, or English and German. Most people, however, explained these likenesses in what seemed to them a logical manner, namely, that one of the languages was the oldest, and that the others were its descendants. Sir William Jones, in his famous address of 1786, was one of the first to question the validity of this widespread belief, and Rasmus Rask went a step further by devising a method for arriving at the nature and degree of this relationship, established—so he determined—when the agreement between words was so consistent that rules could be drawn up for summarizing the shift in "letters" from one language to another. Jacob Grimm confirmed, enlarged upon, and systematized Rask's statement. In the first volume of the second edition (1822) of his *Grammar*, he cites lists of words from various languages, demonstrating thereby the regularity of the phonetic correspondences between the Germanic languages and other non-Germanic yet obviously related tongues. So regular are the correspondences, that Grimm was able to set up a series of formula-like statements to which a later generation applied the term "laws."

Grimm's "Law," however, amounts to considerably more than a set of phonetic correspondences relating Germanic to the Indo-European family of languages. Indeed, as far as essential factual information is concerned, Grimm scarcely improved upon the findings of Rask. The German's real contribution lies rather in the theory he put forward in order to explain the systematic "shifts" in the consonantism from Primitive Indo-European to Primitive Germanic and, subsequently, to Old High German. His explanation was the first of several such theoretical inquiries into the causes of sound change that led scholars a few decades later to make the revolutionary pronouncement that "sound laws are without exception." Because of its importance in the history of linguistics, we shall devote a few pages to a discussion of Grimm's Law.

Grimm coined a special term to describe the complex of interrelated phonetic changes whereby almost the entire stock of Germanic consonants developed from corresponding (but not the same!) Indo-European consonants. The term is "sound shift"— *Lautverschiebung*. Scholars today refer to the "Germanic Sound

Shift," which—in the only slightly exaggerated words of the late Eduard Prokosch—"is probably the most comprehensive group of sound changes that has been observed in the history of any language."

As established by Rask and Grimm, this shift involved all the stops and spirants of Indo-European (with a single exception to be noted later). Rask's immediate purpose in pointing up these correspondences was to establish the relationship between Greco-Latin and Germanic; he does not include examples from the Sanskrit. Grimm wanted to compare all the Germanic languages with one another and, on a grander scale, also demonstrate their relationship to the "Aryan" or Indo-European family of languages. He quotes more copiously than Rask, especially from German, for—as we shall see—he sought to extend the dynamics of the Germanic consonant shift and thereby account for another series of phonetic changes that resulted centuries later in the emergence of a new set of German dialects known collectively as Old High German. For this reason, certain scholars who share this persuasion with Grimm sometimes use the terms "First Sound Shift" and "Second Sound Shift." The two shifts are better referred to as the "Germanic" and the "Old High German," respectively.

Limiting our remarks for the time being to Germanic, the following sets of words may serve as illustrations of what Grimm meant by "correspondences" between Indo-European (as represented by Greek) and Germanic (as represented by Gothic—that Germanic language for which we possess the oldest sizable body of evidence).

Greek	Gothic
*po*ùs (gen. *podós*)	*f*ōtus 'foot'
*t*reîs	*þ*reis 'three'
*k*ardíā	*h*airtō 'heart'
———	———
*d*éka	*t*aihun 'ten'
*g*énos	*k*uni 'race'
*ph*érō	*b*airan 'bear'
*th*ygátēr	*d*auhtar 'daughter'
*ch*órtos	*g*ards 'yard'

To the italic letters in the preceding examples, Grimm assigned approximately the following sound-values (the symbols are assumed to be *phonetic* transcriptions; see the Table of Phonetic Symbols, page 99, for an interpretation):

Greek	Gothic
p	f
t	θ
k	χ
—	—
d	t
g	k
f	b
θ	d
χ	g

Using the terminology of his day, Grimm employed the following terms for the three series of consonants under discussion:

Grimm's Terminology	Modern Terminology
Tenues (p, t, k)	Voiceless stops
Mediae (b, d, g)	Voiced stops
Aspiratae (f, θ, χ)	Voiceless spirants

The classes of sounds within each series he termed "labial, dental, guttural." Modern phoneticians prefer the words "palatal" or "velar" to "guttural." The term "velar" is used in this book.

It will be noted that the chart shows two blank spaces: the labial class of the central set of series is missing. The reason for this is that neither Rask nor Grimm was able to find convincing examples of such a correspondence (b–p) between Greco-Latin and Germanic. Rask erred—probably out of caution—by simply assuming that IE [b], if it existed, had continued unchanged in Germanic. Grimm, largely by deduction rather than from evidence, ventured to establish the missing correspondence, but only when the "letters" occurred in medial position (as in the pair: Greek *kannabis*—Old Norse *hampr*). Grimm reasoned that, according to the pattern of the phonetic correspondences, Germanic words containing ortho-

graphic *p* should be traceable to IE cognates with *b* (or its equivalent, depending upon the alphabet employed). But all his examples
(and Rask's) were in words that either had been borrowed, or for
which no IE cognates could be established. The single exception
was the one just quoted: the Greek word for "hemp," *kannabis*.
Therefore, concluded Grimm, since Germanic preserves no etymologically verifiable [p] in initial position, that could only mean that
Indo-European had had no initial [b]. Since, however, he had one
clear example of a *medial* Germanic [p] for which an IE cognate in
[b] could be found, he felt justified in adding the missing correspondence, but only with the qualification that its distribution in
the parent language was limited to medial position.

As a matter of fact, there are almost no instances of the voiced
bilabial stop that can unequivocally be called Indo-European, since
most of the cognates are limited either to Balto-Germanic (Lithuanian *dubùs* "deep"—Gothic *diups* "deep") or Slavo-Germanic (Old
Bulgarian *slabŭ* "slack"—Gothic *slēpan* "to sleep"). In any event,
although Grimm's intuitive deduction proved to be essentially correct, it may be questioned whether the facts at his disposal war-
ranted the conclusion.

As the chart also shows, Grimm assigned the phonetic values [f],
[θ], and [χ] to the Greek letters *φ, ϑ, χ*; that is, he took them to
stand for voiceless spirants. It might also be mentioned that he
accorded spirantal pronunciation to their Latin transliterations:
the digraphs *ph, th,* and *ch.* Probably most classicists assume that
the Greek symbols, certainly in all the earlier dialects, reflect
aspirated voiceless stops (as in English *pan, tan, can*), although
whether we must posit for Indo-European a series of either voiced
or voiceless aspirated stops wherever Greek shows *φ, ϑ, χ* is still
debatable. In any event, Grimm could not be expected to have
known this. He assumed that a series of IE voiceless spirants
("aspiratae") became in Germanic a corresponding series of voiced
stops ("mediae"); in the latter instance he took orthographic *b,
d, f* to stand for phonetic [b], [d], [g], an assumption that derived

from his consistent failure to distinguish between letters and sounds. This weakness introduced the following error into his conclusions.

In his study of the Germanic verb, Grimm had observed in different inflectional forms of the same word an apparent inconsistency in the "spelling":

Preterite Singular	Preterite Plural
Gothic *þarf*	*þaurbum* 'needed'
Old Saxon *lēth*	*lidun* 'went'
Gothic *aih*	*aigun** 'own'

* *aihan* 'to have' is a so-called preterite-present, that is, a verb that is preterite in form but present in meaning.

Thus, instead of an expected *f*, *þ*, or *h* from an Indo-European *p*, *t*, *k*, the Germanic witnesses sometimes showed *b*, *d*, *g*. But not always. Old English *weorþan* "become" has as its preterite plural *wurdon*, but Gothic records no such change: *wairþan–waurþum*. To this interplay between aspiratae and mediae in the verbal system Grimm gave the name "grammatical change" (*grammatischer Wechsel*). What he failed to discern, as we shall take up a bit later, was that, depending upon the location of the stress-accent in Indo-European, [p], [t], [k] became in Germanic *either* the voiceless spirants [f], [θ], [χ], *or* the voiced spirants [β], [ð], [γ]. Ignoring certain technical considerations, we may say that at least two factors obscured this development: (1) the extent to which analogy had "leveled" the phonetic differences between the preterite singular and plural; and (2) the lack of specific symbols for indicating in writing the presence of the voiced spirants. An additional factor of a slightly different nature is that the voiced spirants tended to become voiced stops in the later stages of most of the Germanic languages and dialects.

Grimm was not especially disturbed by such instances of what seemed to him to be irregular phonetic developments. After all, *he* never applied the word "law" to the series of correspondences he had observed between Indo-European and Germanic. Nor would he have subscribed to a later statement that sound laws are not subject to exceptions, for he believed that provision always had to be made for irregularities: "A sound shift is generally valid, but never clean-cut" (*Die lautverschiebung erfolgt in der masse, thut sich aber im einzelnen niemahls rein ab*). The accentual conditions regulating the dual development of the IE voiceless stops in Germanic would not be determined for another fifty years, and it seems pointless and rather petty when certain writers of a later generation berate Grimm for "misrepresenting" the facts, or for having been "unscientific."

Up to this point Grimm had made no appreciable advance beyond Rask. True, he had expanded and organized the material, presented the results in tabular form, and thereby had given to the whole a perspicuity that is missing in Rask's almost laconic treatment. But this, too, had actually been done a year earlier (1821) by one of Rask's countrymen, Jakob Bredsdorff, in a monograph entitled *On the Causes of Change in Language*. In order to appreciate Grimm's distinctly unique contribution to comparative linguistics, we must extend the scope of the Germanic Consonant Shift to include those sound changes usually subsumed under the term "The High German Sound Shift."

Briefly put, the High German Shift is this: the Germanic voiceless stops [p], [t], [k] became voiceless spirants [f], [θ], [χ] in medial or final position, but affricates ("a stop plus a homorganic spirant") —[pf], [ts], [kχ]—in initial or post-consonantal position. These changes took place to a varying degree in the dialects spoken throughout Middle and Upper Germany (including Austria and part of Switzerland), resulting in a linguistic cleavage that divided into two districts what had been a relatively homogeneous speech area: Primitive German. Those dialects affected by the above-mentioned sound shifts are reckoned to the High German group; those unaffected by these changes are classified as "Low German." The words "high" and "low" referred originally to elevation above sea level, the Low German dialects being spoken chiefly in the flat-lands of northern Germany, giving way gradually to High German dialects in the increasingly mountainous terrain of the central and southern areas.

In tabular arrangement, the High German Shift may be presented as follows:

GERMANIC (as represented by Old Saxon)	Medial Position	OLD HIGH GERMAN
o*p*an		o*ff*an 'open'
e*t*an		e*ss*an 'eat'
ma*k*on		ma*ch*ōn 'make'
	Initial Position	
*p*und		*pf*unt 'pound'
*t*ehan		*z*ehan 'ten'
*k*ō		*ch*ō 'cow'

The phonetic equivalents of the italic letters are:

	Medial Position	
p	becomes	f
t	becomes	s
k	becomes	χ
	Initial Position	
p	becomes	pf
t	becomes	ts
k	becomes	kχ

Although Grimm's interpretation of the phonetic values to be attached to the letters agrees in the main with this chart, his unfortunate use of the term "aspirate" to include at times both spirants *and* affricates robs his presentation of the necessary accuracy. Even if patently erroneous, his faulty practices are at least understandable when we bear in mind the general inability of his age to separate sound and letter. His long chapter on phonology, you will recall, bears the title "Study of the Letters." And the letters of the Old German manuscripts, reflecting divergent spelling traditions as well as dialectal differences, presented a most confusing situation. We must remember that Grimm had no carefully edited texts to guide him, but more often than not had to struggle with the chaotic orthography of the manuscripts, an orthography in which [pf] is usually written *ph; z* is used for both [ts] and [s]; and [χ] is recorded as *h, ch, hc, hcch,* and *hch* (to mention only the more common spellings). Due largely to such scribal vagaries as these, Grimm was again content to tolerate an abundance of apparent exceptions to the Old High German sound shift, although under the circumstances his sins are indeed venial.

As Grimm studied these two shifts—the Germanic and the Old High German—he became aware of what seemed to him to be a fundamental principle at work; a principle that joined together the two processes in a remarkable but reasonable manner. From this point on, Jacob Grimm is not directly indebted to any of the earlier workers—or, for that matter, to any of his contemporaries. In its simplest form, this fundamental principle may be represented by the diagram in Figure 1.

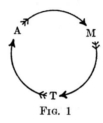

Fig. 1

Grimm used the term *Kreislauf* ("revolution, circulation") to describe the progression of the tenues (T), aspiratae (A), and mediae (M) in their transition from Indo-European to Germanic to Old High German (see chart on p. 29). Referring to the charts on pages 22–23, it is obvious that in the change from Indo-European to Germanic each of the three series of consonants progressed through one stage or phase of the cycle. The misleading term "aspirate" must of course be interpreted to mean "spirant."

The High German consonant shift (p. 27), according to Grimm, completed the cycle, whereby each consonantal series in Germanic moved through another phase of the circle, thus completing the triad. It is by way of illustrating this final stage that his loose and sometimes inaccurate phonetic interpretations are most obvious. By letting "aspirate" serve as a catch-all expression for both spirant and affricate, he is able to cite correspondences testifying to the validity of his *Kreislauf* principle. It should be added, however, that in order to demonstrate the AMT stage, Grimm refers to a High German development not shown on page 27, namely, the change of [b], [d], [g] to [p], [t], [k] in Upper German dialects: Middle German *berg, dohter, guot*—Upper German *perk, tohter, kōt*. And in the TAM cycle he assigns occlusive pronunciation to *b, d, g,* whereas we know the symbols frequently stood for spirants (pp. 25–26).

Rearranging the two sound shifts in terms of their progression through the cycle, we get the following scheme:

Indo-European	T	M	A
Germanic	A	T	M
Old High German	M	A	T
Examples:			
Greek	phrā́*t*ōr	*d*éka	*th*ygátēr
Gothic	brō*þ*ar	*t*aihan	*d*auhtar
Old High German	bruo*d*er	*z*ehan	*t*ohter

Of importance to us is that this marks the first time that anyone had sought to establish a governing principle underlying a complex of phonetic changes. This was something new and important. Rask and others had perceived the workings, but it was Jacob Grimm who first posited the principle which co-ordinated these discrete changes, bringing them together as phases of one grand process. That his explanation may not be completely accurate is of little importance; of much greater significance was its value for all future research in historical and comparative linguistics. Scholars came to realize that sound-change was not haphazard, but was apparently regulated by certain "laws." This gave them incentive to suspect and look for some sovereign principle underlying other instances of language-change. Not that they would always solve the puzzle, but the principle was now established that languages, too, are subject to certain discernible forces, and the effects of these forces so permeate a language that what at first glance seems like an assortment of unrelated changes, in fact turns out to constitute a pattern.

Jacob Grimm did much more than tabulate a series of consonant

changes; *he set forth the conditions governing those changes.* We know
that some of what he said was based upon inadequate or inaccurate
information. But his was the vision, and his greatness should not
be denied him. He saw through to principles and patterns. And this
was the step that had to be taken to prepare the way for the science
of historico-comparative linguistics and—in our own day—structural linguistics.

The increased interest in and knowledge of Sanskrit soon led
scholars to attempt comparative studies of much broader scope.
Indeed, Indo-European comparative linguistics had its true beginnings only when approached through the Sanskrit. The scholar
most responsible for widening the base of comparative grammar to
include the indispensable Indic and Iranian was another German
professor, Franz Bopp (1791–1867). In 1833 began appearing his
monumental *Comparative Grammar of Sanskrit, Zend, Greek, Latin,
Lithuanian, Gothic and German* (*Vergleichende Grammatik des
Sanskrit, Zend, Griechischen, Litthauischen, Gothischen und Deut-
schen*). The grammar was completed in 1852, and two later editions
appeared in 1857 and 1868. To the languages mentioned in the
original title, Bopp later added analyses of Old Slavic, Celtic, and
Albanian.

Bopp's chief interest was in morphology, and in this respect he
differed radically from Rask and Grimm, both of whom were
essentially concerned with phonetic change (as they understood it).
Not only does Bopp attempt an analysis of the composition of
words, but, after isolating the inflectional elements, he tries to trace
them in turn back to their original form and meaning. In this—the
announced intention of his work—he was eminently *un*successful,
since today we must reject almost every one of his explanations.
He was led by a romantic compulsion to look for some form of the
word "to be" in every verb. A sentence, he reasoned, is basically a
subject and an object coupled together by a verbal element. Since
the function of the verb is to relate the subject to the object (actor–
action–thing acted upon), then the only true verb is the so-called

copulative or substantive, namely, the verb "to be." He uses the Latin *potest* as an illustration. This verbal form may be translated "he, she, or it is able," or, in a slightly figurative sense, "it is possible." Bopp points out that this one word is really a complete sentence: The final *t* signifies the third person singular and serves as the subject; the *-es-* is the copulative, meaning "is"; and the object is the root *pot-*, which has the basic meaning of "power." Thus, "he is power" equals "he is able."

Bopp was a Sanskritist by training, and the methods of word-analysis he uses are those by means of which a Sanskrit "word" is resolved into its parts. As discussed earlier, the principles of juncture (*sandhi*) in Sanskrit are so regular, and the morphological constituents so transparent, that the student of the language gains a clear insight into the processes of word-formation and, consequently, wins new understanding of the origin and function of grammatical categories.

Although Bopp's prejudiced and fanciful theories robbed his results of any lasting worth, his new technique of analysis and his demonstration of the obvious value of Sanskrit in comparative studies secured for him a high degree of recognition and influence. Linguistics without Sanskrit could not have gone much beyond Rask, and, although Bopp did little more than illustrate its usefulness, the full potential of this ancient language was finally recognized. The way was now clear for a truly comparative study of those languages whose relationship had been established at least provisionally. In 1861 such a study appeared. It was written by the greatest methodologist of nineteenth-century linguistics, August Schleicher (1821–68).

Schleicher was interested in three subjects: philosophy, natural science, and linguistics. As a student at Tübingen he became an ardent Hegelian, later in his life he was strongly influenced by Charles Darwin, and in his last years he sought, by a synthesis of Hegel's theory of history and Darwin's theory of natural selection, to present a logical and demonstrable theory of language.

His *Compendium of Comparative Grammar of Indo-European Languages* (*Compendium der vergleichenden Grammatik der indogermanischen Sprachen*)—the work referred to above—is a well-organized, clearly written account based almost completely upon the investigations of other scholars. Schleicher discovered little if anything that was new, but he had a brilliant, orderly, and consistently logical mind. Furthermore, he commanded a vigorous, forthright style, and achieved a lucidity of expression seldom matched by other writers in his field. As a result, his grammar was for years a recognized and authoritative text.

Schleicher's three most notable contributions to linguistics are his theory of language relationship, his "comparative method" of reconstructing a parent language, and his classification of languages into types (taxonomy).

He believed so strongly in the independent, lifelike development of languages that he did not hesitate to trace their relationship in approximately the same manner in which a botanist classifies plants. If he found that two languages exhibited certain similar characteristics, he concluded that they had undergone a period of mutual development, much as the botanist will assign to the same genus two species of flowers sharing certain similar features. By carrying this analysis back far enough, he arrived at a point where further subdividing or branching was empirically impossible. The sum of all such comparisons, reasoned Schleicher, was the *Ursprache*—the primitive or original language; not the *first* language of mankind—there was no way to ascertain that—but the oldest ancestor of a given "family" of languages. In fact, he refers specifically to the Indo-European "family tree" (*Stammbaum*), and drew up a genealogical chart in which he plotted the relationship of all these languages.

Schleicher's procedure is open to a number of serious objections. Theoretically, of course, this method of comparison yields a dialect-free *Ursprache*, for if a language is reconstructed only from samenesses, obviously it will possess no variants. In practice, however, we know that no speech-community is ever completely free of dialectal forms. Nor was Indo-European. In trying to determine the case-forms of substantives in the parent language, for instance, we cannot reach agreement on the form of the inflectional suffix used to mark one of the oblique cases of the plural, for regardless of how many periods of mutual development we posit, we are left with not one but two suffixes, both clearly attested to, both amply documented, and both equally ancient. Cases of this sort are numerous and permit of only one conclusion: Indo-European, like any other language, had dialectal variants. The comparative method, however, in theory does not admit this possibility, because it assumes that each language bears independent witness to the forms of the parent language, and that correspondences among the related languages guarantee those features—and *only* those features—in the parent speech.

A corollary of this assumption is that a parent language split suddenly and completely into two or more daughter languages, and that these siblings from the moment of cleavage had no further contact with one another. This assumption is methodologically necessary, for if we were to admit that similarities between two or more languages could be due to mutual *influence* rather than to mutual *development*, we would then have no way at all of deriving historical relationships. Of course, we know that languages frequently do continue to influence one another long after they have developed into discrete linguistic entities. It would be pointless to say that Dutch and German have not influenced one another, or that there has been no linguistic give-and-take between Swedish and Danish, or Polish and Russian. Here again, the premises of the comparative method are palpably false.

If, then, this method of determining relationships between languages is based upon such erroneous assumptions, why is it still used? The answer is: Because *as a method* it works quite well. The linguist proceeds *as if* the assumptions were valid, goes as far as the method allows, then sets about correcting his results in the light of all available information. The gas laws of physical chemistry offer a roughly analogous situation. In actual practice one must always correct for variations from "standard" temperature and pressure, otherwise the results are not accurate. The basic formula for computing the rate of movement of a body must always include a correction for friction. And so it is with the comparative method. Once we correct for certain obvious errors, we find that it functions rather well; better, certainly, than any other method yet proposed. We have rejected most of Schleicher's theories, but we have retained the essential features of his method.

Certain archeological discoveries from around the turn of the last century have raised additional doubts as to the intrinsic reliability of the comparative method. Most notable of these was the unearthing in southeastern Asia Minor of cuneiform tablets in a language which, upon decipherment, showed striking similarities to Indo-European, especially to the Celtic and Italic branches. This language is Hittite. Because of its great antiquity (the Hittite empire flourished from about 2000 to 1200 B.C.), and because it is in certain respects quite different from what was then believed to have been the form of Primitive Indo-European, some scholars at first proposed that Hittite and Indo-European were both descended from an earlier stage that they called Proto-Indo-Hittite. Although this theory has been largely abandoned, and Hittite is now considered to be simply one of the oldest of the Indo-European languages, its sometimes striking divergencies from the anticipated pattern strongly suggested the possibility of faulty methods of reconstruction; for Proto-Indo-European as reconstructed by the comparative method is of a highly synthetic nature, possessing a rich and elaborate set of inflectional affixes, whereas Hittite tends to be more analytic in structure, displaying somewhat less inflection. This disparity posed an obvious problem: Why the elaborate morphology in the reconstructed language? Although the disparities between Hittite and Proto-Indo-European have largely disappeared as a result of more careful reconstructions, the answer no doubt still lies to some degree in the fallacy of the propositions upon which the comparative method rests, since it does not allow for varieties in the parent languages or for common changes, independently arrived at, in the related languages. Actually, in order to yield reliable information, the factors of time and space must be subjected to certain controls. If we do not go too far back in time or attempt to cover too broad an area, then we can have confidence in our reconstructions—provided, of course, that we start out with historically attested forms! This has been borne out by applying the method to the Germanic and especially to the Romance language areas, where inscriptions and documents have confirmed the reliability of our results. But where too much time has elapsed and where the areas become too vast, then the "variables" and the "unknowns" can skew our results beyond the limits of tolerance.

An outgrowth of Schleicher's devotion to Hegelian philosophy is his classification of linguistic types. Language, so Schleicher proposed, consists of *meaning* and *form*. Since there is no such thing as a language without meaning, these two basic characteristics of speech permit a threefold division (Hegel's triads). The first division includes those languages in which the grammatical form of the words contributes little or nothing to the total linguistic meaning. A language such as Chinese serves as an example, since, aside from the position of the word in the sentence, there are few distinctions between grammatical categories. The sentence: "Steam boat blows whistle" may serve as an example. Each of these words can be used in English both as a noun and as a verb. Of course, we add an -*s* to *blow* when the subject is third person singular—which Chinese would not do—but otherwise the meaning of the words is dependent upon their position in the sentence. Schleicher used the term "isolating" to describe a tongue of this type.

The second classification embraces those idioms in which the linguistic units incorporate both lexical and structural meaning, but in which the formative processes are very obvious and the formative elements are constant. Schleicher called this group "agglutinative"; Turkish is usually mentioned as the classic example. English compound words such as "statehood," "ladylike," and "manageable" are crudely analogous. The identifying features of this linguistic type are that the root-word is invariable, the juncture between the root and its suffixed components is clearly discernible, and the additive elements have independent meaning.

Third, there are those languages in which meaning and form are synthesized (Hegel's thesis, antithesis, synthesis) or fused together. Not only is the root itself capable of internal modification (e.g., *sing–sang–sung*) but, in addition, the form may be further modified by prefixes, infixes, and suffixes, the use of which always results in a constant change in meaning. Of significance to Schleicher, the independent meaning of the various affixes and the sutures joining them to a root have become quite obscure in this third group of languages, the so-called "inflectional," of which Latin and Greek are excellent examples. The first person singular, present indicative of the verb "to be" in Gothic is *im*. The speaker of Gothic was doubtless quite unaware that this verb-form contained the phonetic reflexes of what, in the Indo-European parent language, had been two morphemes: a root *es* meaning "be, exist," and a suffix -*mi*, which was at one time most likely a pronoun of the first person singular. The Sanskrit equivalent of "(I) am"—*asmi*—shows quite clearly the probable development of this form of the verb "to be."

As a student of the natural sciences, Schleicher was keenly aware of the life-cycle of all cellular organisms: birth, maturity, old age, and death. When the body reaches that stage in its development where regeneration cannot keep pace with degeneration, atrophy and decay are the result. Coupled to this observation was Schleicher's acceptance of Hegel's theory of history, a belief that all progress is but a constant interplay of opposing forces (called "dialectic") and the successful or unsuccessful merging of these forces. Hegel used the terms "thesis," "antithesis," and "synthesis." Schleicher combined these products of scientific and philosophic thought to formulate his own theory of language.

Language, he deduced, must have first been of an isolating nature (thesis). This is the simplest, most naïve type of structure. Then it progressed to the agglutinative stage, a slightly more complex, more intellectual manner of expression which, with its emphasis on form, served as the antithesis. Finally, man's mental prowess and advanced capacity for logic permitted him to make the ultimate synthesis between meaning and form, and language thus reached the inflectional level. Applying this reasoning to languages as he found them round about him, Schleicher posed the obvious question: At what point are we in the life-cycle of our Indo-European languages? The answer was patent. The zenith of linguistic development coincided with the maximum of inflectional ability. As Schleicher had traced the Indo-European languages back on their family tree, he discovered that the older the language, the more inflection it showed. Latin, then Greek, and finally Sanskrit with its lavish abundance of declensions and conjugations—this was the path which the linguist retraced in his probings back into the past. Everything (so he thought) pointed to the strong probability that the "mother tongue"—Proto-Indo-European—had been richer in inflection than any of its many offspring. Where, then, did the historical languages belong in the linguistic life-cycle? Clearly in the period of decay and degeneration. Sanskrit and the classical tongues were still close to their full vigor, whereas a language so shorn of inflection as, say, English, was in a sad state indeed!

To what extent does history bear out Schleicher's philosophically inspired theory of language development? Is there any evidence supporting his contention that language developed through the three stages of isolation, agglutination, and inflection? Since the last two steps are in a broad sense but phases of a single process—the juncture of smaller meaningful units—it is highly probable that certain forms did originate simply by joining together independent semantic units. Unfortunately, however—and this is important—there is little direct evidence to bolster this supposition. Many linguists, for instance, assume that the personal endings of the verb were at one time full-fledged pronouns and that the case-endings of nouns were once prepositions. Actually, though, this conclusion is reached solely by inference. As far back as they can be traced, the verbal and nominal suffixes have no independence; they are not "words" in their own right. Likewise, the historicity of an original isolating-type language is not demonstrable. The idea is logical enough to warrant probability, but the written records of the Indo-European languages grant no confirmation. There is, furthermore, no factual basis for considering an isolating language "primitive." Why is it primitive? Because it lacks formal markers which set apart the dative from the ablative case? Isolating languages such as Chinese are capable of intricate and artistic expression rivaling and sometimes surpassing that of the touted inflectional tongues. The familiar pidginized version of Chinese speech-patterns ("Number one boy go chop-chop bring Missee tea") does indeed sound primitive to our ears, but only because the *English* sentence is shorn of its normal and native devices for indicating syntactic units. Curiously enough, most Sinologists apparently believe the prehistoric structure of Chinese to have been quite complex. If this is true, then its isolating structure is anything but primitive.

In spite of all these shortcomings, however, Schleicher's influence has endured until now. A modified version of his comparative method is still employed, and most comparative linguists will still accept a reconstruction labeled "Proto-Indo-European." His classification of languages into isolating, agglutinative, and inflectional (the idea was not original with Schleicher; both Wilhelm von Humboldt and August Pott, a German etymologist of note, had proposed similar schemes as early as the 1830's) is no longer considered adequate by most workers, although the terms are still used to describe the respective processes. His life-cycle interpretation of the growth of language is even today believed by perhaps the majority of people —including scholars—although a modest amount of reflection ought to reveal its unwarranted basis. Language is not an organism; it does not decay. Language *changes*—that is all we can say.

Schleicher was predominantly concerned with the morphology of languages, since he felt that the grammatical structure was that feature of a language least subject to extraneous forces and there-fore most likely to have preserved its integrity. Even the sounds he considered less stable and more liable to be changed by such non-linguistic forces as migration, conquest, and the like. Since he considered vocabulary to be the most volatile ingredient of a linguistic system (as indeed it is), he attached little importance to it as evidence of kinship between languages. The task of trying to establish the vocabulary of the Indo-European prototype, therefore, was undertaken by another scholar—August Fick (1833–1916)—whose *Comparative Dictionary of the Indo-European Languages* (*Vergleichendes Wörterbuch der indogermanischen Sprachen*) first appeared in 1868. A third edition, greatly expanded, was published in the years 1874–76; a fourth edition, begun in 1890, was never completed.

Fick's dictionary is important to us because it was the first major attempt to apply to vocabulary Schleicher's family-tree theory for determining language relationships. Establishing two broad divisions into Indo-Iranian and Common European (which yielded the vocabulary of the Indo-European parent language), Fick next posited a cleavage of the latter group into two separate branches, Southern European (Greco-Italic) and Northern European (Germanic-Baltic-Slavic). Finally, he further subdivided the Northern European entity into a Germanic branch and a Balto-Slavic branch. All this proceeded according to the premise laid down by Schleicher that samenesses between any two languages may be assumed to stem from a period of mutual development, whereas the differences arose independently after this proto-language had divided. Thus, in order for a word to find its way into the Indo-European parent language, its occurrence would have to be documented in a language belonging to both the Indo-Iranian and the Common European groups. A word recorded only in Greek and Latin, however, would be limited to the Southern European proto-language.

Here again, although today we still follow this general method of establishing the vocabulary of the proto-language, we have rejected the Schleicher-Fick theory. Genetic relationship among languages cannot consistently be plotted in the way we construct genealogical charts. Such a method of establishing linguistic affinities can only apply in those cases where a linguistic stock has been suddenly and permanently split by migrations, whereas we know that many similarities between languages must be attributed to diffusion from a central source. Etymologists of today, therefore, are not at all content merely to tally up the languages in which a given word occurs, note which branches of the genealogical chart are represented, and then categorically assign the word to this or that proto-language. A word shared by all witnesses except Indo-Iranian, for instance, might very well be reckoned to the Proto-Indo-European vocabulary, whereas an item shared only by Indo-Iranian and, say, Greek (Southern European), would in general probably be denied such status. The point is, reconstruction of any part of a linguistic system is an extremely complicated process for which there is no neat set of operations that can be mechanically applied. Fick, however, even in the finished portions of the fourth edition of his *Dictionary*, adhered to his original tenet that a word had to be found in Indo-Iranian *and* Common European in order to be included in the Proto-Indo-European vocabulary. Nevertheless, in spite of its serious limitations, his work marks another milestone in the history of linguistics, because here again we see an attempt to apply a principle to a mass of data and, by its application, bring order into what was largely random observation and description.

Fick's dictionary has in some ways never been equaled, although it was eventually superseded by a work compiled by Alois Walde and Julius Pokorny (*Vergleichendes Wörterbuch der indogermanischen Sprachen*), published from 1927 to 1932. A new lexicon (which began to appear in 1947), based to a large extent upon the old one but incorporating the findings of more recent scholarship, was completed in 1960. Julius Pokorny was its compiler.

We now approach what in many ways must be considered the most significant decade in the history of modern linguistics—the 1870's—for during these years the thesis, earlier announced by Jacob Grimm, that there is a principle uniting, underlying, and lending pattern to sound-changes came to be applied with spectacular results. During this decade the scientific study of language came into its own.

August Schleicher, for all his many contributions, had in certain fundamental areas worked—unwittingly of course—to retard progress in comparative studies. The reason is simple: he was so concerned with proving and maintaining a theory that he would not let the facts speak for themselves. He could not, for instance, countenance any evidence that pointed to what he considered "decay" in the parent language, for that was the Golden Age when the words were still "undamaged in all their parts." Furthermore, he was committed to accept Sanskrit as reflecting a stage of linguistic development only slightly removed in excellence and purity from the mother tongue. As an example of how this slavish devotion to doctrine introduced a gross error into his teachings, we might consider briefly his concept of the Indo-European vowel system.

Schleicher proposed three vowels for the parent language: *a, i, u* (both long and short in quantity). His choice was dictated by Sanskrit, which shows the same pattern, as does—according to his interpretation—the Gothic. Although the details cannot be discussed here, suffice it to say that his assumption made utterly impossible any systematic derivation of the IE vowel system based upon the comparative evidence of the historical languages; he was obliged to accept a bewildering array of "exceptions" that he had to attribute to countless independent developments, sporadic and haphazard changes or lack of change, and so forth. When other scholars suggested that vowels might have "weakened" or "dropped out" under certain conditions in Indo-European, Schleicher would have none of it, for such processes seemed too much like "decay" to him. When confronted with examples of the principal parts of certain Greek verbs like *petomai* "I fly," *pepotēmai, eptomēn* (note the root syllable: *pet, pot, pt*), in which the third form apparently lacks a root vowel, he steadfastly refused to admit that this loss could have taken place in the parent language, but, because this was evidence of damage and mutilation, he assigned it to a period of independent development in Greek. The fact that this sort of pattern in the principal parts of Greek verbs has a consistent parallel throughout the daughter languages failed to sway him. He would not tolerate "corruption" in the parent language. Any syllable, in order to be granted Indo-European status, had to have as its resonant element the phonetic counterpart of *a*, *i*, or *u*.

But the old order was changing. The lesson of the Germanic and Old High German consonant shifts had been too well learned. One after another, in the seventies, there appeared a series of brilliant writings by other and mostly younger scholars proving conclusively that Schleicher's Indo-European vowel triad was a myth. And the proof was arrived at by a careful examination of the facts, trying all the while to define the conditions governing and regulating the seemingly unrelated and different phonological changes.

Scholars had long noted that Sanskrit frequently had the palatal [č]—usually given as *c* in transliteration—where other related languages show a voiceless labiovelar sound. Thus: Skt. -*ca*—Latin -*que;* Skt. *pañca*—Latin *quinque.* In other situations, however, Sanskrit too recorded a velar stop: Skt. *kas*—Latin *quod.* On the strength of these and many other examples, several scholars (more or less independently) arrived at the correct interpretation of the evidence: Wherever Sanskrit showed the palatalized stop [č], other witnesses had preserved the voiceless labiovelar [kʷ] *followed by a front vowel, usually spelled* e; and when Sanskrit showed an initial *k*-plus orthographic *a*, other languages had symbols for a voiceless labiovelar stop [kʷ] plus [o]. The conclusion was obvious that the parent language—as well as Sanskrit at some time in its early history—had had the vowels [e] and [o] as well as [a], [i], [u].

This is just one of a series of observations made at that time which resulted in a drastic revision of the vocalism and consonantism of Schleicher's reconstructed Indo-European. Not only was the vowel structure increased to include [e] and [o], but in 1876 Karl Brugmann published a famous article claiming that the nasal and liquid consonants, written *m*, *n*, *r*, and *l*, could also function as resonants, thus introducing the principle of syllabic [m̥], [n̥], [l̥], [r̥]. Although his reconstruction of these "syllabics" has been questioned by certain scholars (especially his assumption of a series of "long" syllabics in Indo-European), he did demonstrate quite conclusively the presence of certain unaccented vowels in the parent language—and that these vowels were of a quality and quantity other than the vowels of the stressed syllables.

The consonantism proposed by Schleicher also came in for considerable revision. He had posited only three "gutturals" for Indo-European: the unaspirated voiceless stop [k], and an unaspirated and aspirated voiced stop, [g] and [g']. Largely as an outgrowth of the efforts to state precisely under what conditions Sanskrit *a* reflected an earlier [a], [o], or [e], the inventory of Indo-European "gutturals" was now increased by nine to include three series: a velar series, a labiovelar series, and a palatal series. Each series in turn consisted of four classes: an unaspirated and aspirated *voiceless* stop, and an unaspirated and aspirated *voiced* stop. Of the several men who worked in this area, we may mention the Italian scholar Graziadio Ascoli, the Dane Vilhelm Thomsen, the Swiss savant Ferdinand de Saussure, and the German Hermann Collitz.

Of the many studies devoted to the reconstruction of Proto-Indo-European phonology, none was more important than a monograph by Ferdinand de Saussure entitled *A Study of the Primitive Vowel System of the Indo-European Languages* (*Mémoire sur le système primitif des voyelles dans les langues indo-européennes*, dated 1879, although it actually appeared a year earlier). This work not only bears eloquent testimony to the value and soundness of the structural approach to linguistic research, but it also teaches us the importance of purely theoretical inquiry in advancing the frontiers of knowledge. Unfortunately, the intellectual climate of the 1870's was so strongly positivistic and empirical that this inspired and ingenious explanation of certain baffling aspects of the Indo-European vowel-system went almost ignored for half a century. Only after Hittite finally became generally accessible to scholars did they realize that there was empirical confirmation of what Saussure had proposed so many years before, and only today is Proto-Indo-European being reconstructed so as to conform to the evidence brought to light by the cuneiform inscriptions from the excavations at Boghaz-köi. I refer to what is known as the "laryngeal theory," ". . . the name commonly given to an assumption made about the phonological system of an early stage of Indo-European. It is assumed that this system included a number of phonemes, usually called laryngeals, of which the various IE dialects show no direct reflexes. . . . Only after Kurylowicz pointed out reflexes of laryngeals in Hittite did Indo-Europeanists generally begin to accept the laryngeal theory" (Winfred P. Lehmann, *Proto-Indo-European Phonology* [Austin: University of Texas Press, 1955], p. 22).

Once the vocalism of Proto-Indo-European had been established to include also [e] and [o], scholars were able to perceive the remarkable system of vowel-alternations that prevailed in the parent language and that is reflected especially well in the "principal parts" of the verb in several of the daughter languages. Jacob Grimm coined the term *Ablaut* to describe this phenomenon; the English term is "mutation," although the German word is acceptable in English as a *terminus technicus*. Consider if you will the following Greek forms:

Present Tense	Perfect Tense	Aorist Tense
ei	*oi*	*i*
peíthō	pépoitha	épithon
('I persuade')		
eu	*ou*	*u*
eleúsomai (fut.)	eiléloutha	éluthon
('I shall go')		
e	*o*	*zero-grade*
pétomai	pepótēmai	eptómēn
('I fly')		

The vowel patterns are fairly obvious: the left-hand and center columns taken together present an *e–o* relationship (*Ei–Oi, Eu–Ou*, in the case of the diphthongs); the right-hand column shows forms in which the *e*-vowel has "disappeared," so that the so-called "normal-grade" diphthongal bases -*ei*- and -*eu*- (*peith*- and *eleuth*-) appear in the "zero-grade" as -*i*- and -*u*-, respectively (-*pith*- and

-luth-). The zero-grade of a monophthongal base like *pet-* of Greek *pétomai* is of course also characterized by the disappearance of the vowel (*-pt-*), thereby losing its syllabic status.

Two types of ablaut are here illustrated. That which is marked by a change in the timbre or quality of the vowel—as between a front and a back vowel (spelled *e* and *o*)—is called "qualitative gradation" or, in German, *Abtönung;* that characterized by a change in the stress or quantity of a vowel—as between the normal-grade and zero-grade of a given vowel—is referred to as "quantitative gradation" or, in German, *Abstufung* (the German terms are highly descriptive). The first-mentioned type supposedly reflects a difference in what must have been a kind of musical pitch that prevailed at some time during the Indo-European period. The second type presumably resulted from the shifts in the stress-accent that occurred in the parent language. Of critical importance to our discussion is that, for whatever reasons, the characteristic vowel of the present tense is *e*, alternating systematically with an *o*-vowel in the perfect tense (ablaut is by no means limited to the verb; it is merely convenient for purposes of illustration to quote verbal forms). In unstressed position, on the other hand, this *e*-vowel is "lost"—at least there is no direct reflex of it preserved in the daughter languages.

Unfortunately, this neat scheme of things is disturbed by certain other ablaut relationships, which—though of less frequency and in a sense of less functional importance in the morphology of Indo-European—must also be accounted for. As for instance the *ā–ō–a* series:

	ā	*ō*	*a*
Greek	phāmí 'I say'	phōnḕ 'voice'	phatós 'said'
	hístāmi 'I put'		statós 'placed'
		dōnum (Latin) 'gift'	datus (Latin) 'given'

To account for this and other relatively infrequent ablaut series, the early Indo-Europeanists constructed an elaborate apparatus. To mention just a few features of it: verbs having a long vowel in a normal-grade root syllable (the quantitative grade that prevails in

most present-tense forms of the IE verb) were said to show a
"heavy base" (such as *phāmí*) to distinguish them from those verbs
containing a "light base" (such as *pétomai*). The short *a*-vowel in
this series was explained as a reflex of the "reduced grade" of a
long vowel, which they represented in the reconstructed Indo-
European form by a special symbol: *ə*, called "shwa" (a term borrowed from Semitic grammar). Phonetically, *ə* is taken to represent
an unstressed central vowel corresponding in a general way to the
pronunciation normally accorded the *e* of *the* in a phrase like "see
the boy."

Without going any deeper into this complex chapter of Indo-
European comparative linguistics, it can be said that a detailed
analysis and explanation along these lines came to be generally accepted. There were many areas of uncertainty and disagreement,
though there were even broader areas of agreement. Most of the
leading scholars of the day tried their hand at an explanation, and
Saussure's detailed monograph was accepted as a brilliant and useful contribution toward a clearer understanding of the intricacies of
the Indo-European ablaut relationships. Nevertheless, hardly anyone seems to have accepted his almost prescient explanation of the
troublesome occurrence of a short *a*-vowel in an ablaut series otherwise characterized by long vowels, such as the *ā–ō–a* series.

Saussure had been especially impressed by the structural pattern
of the most frequently occurring ablaut series: *e* alternating with *o*
on the one hand, and—under specific accentual conditions—
dropping out altogether. Of further significance was that this *e–o*
pair could enter into diphthongal union with *i*, *u*, and—though not
shown in our examples—with the sonants *m*, *n*, *l*, and *r*. Why not,
reasoned Saussure, let this structural pattern serve to explain such
ablaut series as *ā–ō–a? Why not assume that every normally stressed
long vowel had arisen through the contraction of a short vowel with some
unknown phoneme, of which no reflex was to be found in the historical
languages?* Saussure proposed two such phonemes: *A* and *Q*. These
symbols represented laryngeal sonants, the phonetic effect of which
would have been to convert a preceding front vowel into a back

vowel, either *a*-colored or *o*-colored. If, because of lack of stress, the front vowel was lost (zero-grade), then the laryngeal—by definition a sonant—would function vocalically. The orthographic reflection of this function of the laryngeal (in the traditional *ā–ō–a* series) was *a* in all the Indo-European languages save Indic, where it appeared as *i*. Incidentally, Saussure assumed that all normal-grade IE roots had an *e*-vowel.

Although our illustrations must be simplified, it is reasonably accurate to present Saussure's explanation of the effect of the laryngeals on a neighboring vowel in the following schematic fashion:

phāmí	pheAmi
phōnè	pheOnē
phatós	phAtos
hístāmi	histeAmi
statós	stAtos
dōnum	deOnum
datus	dAtus

Structurally this is a brilliant hypothesis, but of course Saussure had no direct evidence with which to bolster his keen proposal. One of the few scholars who adopted his daring explanation was the Dane, Hermann Möller (1850–1923), who, as a specialist in the Semitic languages, gave the name "laryngeals" to the unknown sonants (the sound-system of the Semitic languages is characterized, among other things, by the presence of a series of laryngeal consonants). The name caught on, though the theory as such more or less languished until 1929, when the Polish scholar Jerzy Kurylowicz published an article in which he suggested that the Hittite phoneme *ḫ* (the Akkadian symbol in conventional transliteration) was the reflex of an early Indo-European laryngeal sonant.

The evidence offered by Hittite is not only compelling, but dramatically confirms Saussure's theory. To quote just a few examples: corresponding to Latin *pāscunt* "they protect," West Tocharian *pāskeṃ* "they protect," is Hittite *pasḫanzi* "they protect." Note the *short* vowel followed by the laryngeal in Hittite. Or again:

Greek *neān-*, Latin *novāre*, Hittite *newaḫḫ* "young." Greek *lāos* "army," Hittite *laḫḫa* "war." In such cases as these, the Hittite *ḫ* is interpreted as a reflex of an early Indo-European sonant. The Proto-Indo-European reconstruction would accordingly show a "laryngeal" in the same relative position as Hittite has the *ḫ*.

The laryngeal theory is today one of the most disputed topics in the entire domain of Indo-European comparative linguistics· It is furthermore an exceedingly complicated subject. Much is still theory, although most comparativists now accept as fact that Indo-European did have a certain number of laryngeal sonants. To the extent that Hittite actually shows reflexes of the laryngeals, one can hardly refuse to accept the theory as a valid explanation. To the non-specialist, certainly, the laryngeal theory as first formulated by Ferdinand de Saussure offers a most striking example of the value of theoretical research when pursued by a well-trained and perceptive scholar. And it is of obvious significance to note that it was careful attention to the *total structure* of the Indo-European languages that led Saussure to posit the one-time existence of the laryngeals. That subsequent archeological findings proved the accuracy of his hypothesis simply underscores the importance and the reliability of the structural approach to linguistic problems. The reader who is interested in a full discussion of the laryngeal theory and its application to current linguistic scholarship should consult Winfred P. Lehmann's *Proto-Indo-European Phonology*.

Another instance in the history of linguistics of brilliant and incisive research was a significant discovery made by the Danish scholar, Karl Verner, first made public in 1875 in an article entitled "An Exception to the First Consonant Shift" ("Eine Ausnahme der ersten Lautverschiebung," *Zeitschrift für vergleichende Sprachforschung auf dem Gebiete der indogermanischen Sprachen*, XXIII, 97–130).

Reference has already been made to the confusing development of IE [p], [t], [k] in Germanic: sometimes the documents reflected the "regular" development to voiceless spirants (Sanskrit *bhrātr*—

Gothic *brōþar*), but sometimes the change seemed to be to voiced stops (Sanskrit *pită-* —Gothic *fadar*). Grimm had noticed this, of course, and had been especially impressed by the curious interplay of stop and spirant in the morphology of the strong verb, applying the term "grammatical change" to this phenomenon. But he did not perceive the true reason underlying this dual development. Karl Verner did. Looking to the Sanskrit, the Danish scholar noticed that whenever the accent (which is recorded in Sanskrit texts) fell on the root syllable of the cognate, the Germanic correspondent showed *f*, *þ*, or *h*. When, however, the accent fell on some other syllable, the Germanic equivalents frequently recorded *b*, *d*, or *g*. The Sanskrit-Gothic words for "brother" and "father" given a few lines above may serve as examples (notice the accent mark over the Sanskrit words!). A classic instance is offered by various forms of the Germanic verb "to become," which is a cognate of the Sanskrit "to turn":

Sanskrit	Old English
vártāmi	weorþe 'I become'
vavárta	wearþ 'I became'
vavrtimá	*wurdum 'we became'
vavrtāná	worden 'became' (past participle)

The form with the asterisk does not actually occur. The third person plural of the preterite—*wurdon*—had replaced a regular *wurdum* before the historical period of Old English.

This is the same sort of phonetic change that distinguishes the pronunciation of the letter *x* in the following pairs of English words: *éxit–exáct; éxercise–examíne*. Notice that the shift in stress results in two modifications of the affected consonant-cluster (*x* equals [ks]): it becomes voiced and it is pronounced with less tension of the vocal apparatus (in phonetic transcription: [gz]). In other words, harking back now to the Germanic development of Indo-European [p], [t], [k], what we really have is an interchange between voiceless and voiced *spirants* with a corresponding reduction in tension of articulation, usually described as the difference between *fortis* and *lenis* pronunciation. The difference is not, as Grimm thought, between spirant and stop. This interchange was unevenly carried out (and even less consistently recorded) in the various Germanic languages, but modern scholarship accepts Verner's explanation as correct. It is referred to as "Verner's Law."

Discoveries such as these, based upon careful theoretical considerations and historical evidence, had at least two important results: (1) Both the vocalism and consonantism of the parent language were now reconstructed in a manner more consistent with the facts and with methodological rigor than in accordance with some preconceived and unconfirmable notion. (2) Most of the so-called "exceptions" were found to be simply reflections of a set of circumstances not discernible to earlier workers. Above all, this determined search for causes had convinced many scholars that sound change was not sporadic or haphazard; there *was* an explanation, but it could not be found until valid research procedures conducted with objective precision had replaced a blind adherence to doctrine.

Those scholars who most rigorously—and vociferously!—followed this new direction were dubbed "neogrammarians" (*Junggrammatiker*). In 1876, one of them, the Slavicist August Leskien, coined the now famous phrase: "Sound-laws have no exception" (*Die Ausnahmslosigkeit der Lautgesetze*). Although it is unfortunate that Karl Verner's wording—"No exception without a rule"—could not have caught on instead, it is of lasting importance that a group of able and responsible scholars hereby acknowledged their acceptance of a principle which was to underlie and direct their research, namely, that linguistic change is not haphazard and capricious, but subject to a constant and definable set of conditions; furthermore, that "exceptions" to these conditions are not real but only apparent.

We shall have more to say later on by way of a critical evaluation of this, the neogrammarian position. Suffice it for now to say that the bulk of linguistic research in the United States has received its impetus and direction from scholars trained in the neogrammarian tradition. Of more immediate interest is a discussion of the methods used by the neogrammarians to explain the apparent exceptions to their "laws," especially their reference to *analogy* as a vital factor in linguistic change.

Analogy consists in making things that are alike more alike. Psychologically, it is a simple and obvious type of mental association. Consider the following paradigms of the present indicative active of the Latin verb *amāre* and its phonetic correspondences in Old French and Modern French:

		Classical Latin	Old French	Modern French
Singular	1.	amō	aim	aime
	2.	amās	aimes	aimes
	3.	amat	aime	aime
Plural	1.	amāmus	amons	aimons
	2.	amātis	amez	aimez
	3.	amant	aiment	aiment

The reader's attention is directed to the first and second persons plural of the French examples. The root vowel (spelled *a*) of the Old French forms is the regular phonetic extension of the corresponding unstressed Latin vowel. However, the two forms under discussion— although phonetically quite regular—are at odds with the other members of the paradigm, so that in the course of time they underwent analogical "leveling" in favor of the prevailing pattern. Note, too, that the first person singular of the Modern French has an *e*-ending not present in Old French. This *e* was introduced largely on the analogy of the other persons that had a regular *e* in the terminal syllable, although additional support was lent by certain classes of polysyllabic verbs in which the Latin *ō*-ending had regularly come through as *e* in French.

Or to give a few more examples: In Latin there is a pair of words with contrastive meanings, *gravis* and *levis*, meaning "heavy" and "light," respectively. In spoken Latin there arose a new form, **grevis*. This word was continued in Old French as *gref*, was borrowed by Anglo-Saxon speakers after the Norman Conquest, and lives on as our word *grief*—"heavy" in a figurative sense. Again, in

Attic Greek there is yet another such contrastive pair—*prosthen* and *opisthen*—meaning "in front" and "in back." The *e* of *opisthen* is etymologically unwarranted, as is proved by an earlier *opithen*. Here again, however, analogy caused a leveling in favor of the sibilant, so that classical Greek shows a sigma in both forms.

Although this sort of linguistic change was well known, it was the neogrammarians who first appreciated its relevancy and importance to the scientific study of language. In order properly to assess the value of analogy to them, we must remember their credo: "Sound-laws have no exceptions." They had been led to make this revolutionary pronouncement because time and again some scholar had succeeded in proving that the so-called exceptions to a given phonetic "law" were due to a set of circumstances which had heretofore not been stated with sufficient rigor. Now they realized that many of the often cited irregularities were not at all the result of phonetic change, but dependent upon factors quite outside the province of phonology. These were not exceptions to a sound-law; these were changes explainable in terms of mental association. In analogy, therefore, they found a new and strong ally to support the cardinal tenet of their new science.

While recognizing the effect of mental association on the sounds and forms of language, older scholars had described the process as "*false* analogy," but from their newly found vantage point the neogrammarians realized that there was nothing "false" about it. It was, in fact, an ever present, positive and powerful force in language, responsible for a multitude of changes. And just as sound-changes had been observed to follow certain patterns, so did the changes effected by mental association seem to result from regularizing and normalizing forces constantly at work in language. To the neogrammarian, indeed, the chief factors in the history of language were phonetic change and analogic change. And with this position, contemporary linguistic scholarship in the main agrees.

Before leaving this subject, let us consider a few more examples of how the neogrammarians went about explaining the so-called exceptions to their sound-laws, the *residual forms* (*Restwörter*), as they called them.

There is a phonetic law which, in its original formulation, stated that Proto-Indo-European intervocalic [s] becomes intervocalic [r] in Latin. In the following examples, the word on the left shows a form in which IE [s] has come down unchanged. In the form on the right, the [s] in intervocalic position has changed to [r]:

flōs 'flower'	floris (genitive singular)
genus 'race'	generis (genitive singular)
nefās 'evil' (noun)	nefārius (adjective)
ustus 'burnt'	ūrere 'to burn'

But there are many instances of intervocalic [s] in Latin that seem to pose exceptions to the rule. Words like *mīsī* "I sent" (perfect of *mittere*) or *causa* "cause" may serve as illustrations. However, upon closer scrutiny these exceptions prove to be spurious. *Mīsī*, once its morphology is properly interpreted, can be reconstructed as **mīssī*, which in turn derives from **mitsī;* just as *causa* developed from an earlier *caussa*. The explanation for both of the apparent deviations is that a long consonant, orthographically double *s*, was shortened after a long vowel or diphthong around the beginning of the Christian Era. The words, therefore, are not exceptions to the rule, because at the time when it was in effect they had a long rather than a short consonant intervocalically, a different situation altogether.

Other instances of intervocalic [s] surviving in classical Latin can be explained in different ways. Vocables like *philosophus* and *genesis*, for example, are loan words from Greek, borrowed *after* the Latin sound shift had become inoperative. This particular change had occurred very early in the Italic dialect of Latium (that is, Latin); prior, in fact, to the earliest records, which already show an *r*. Just when the transition took place in Latin we cannot say with certainty. A neighboring Italic dialect records the unshifted intervocalic [s] in about the sixth or seventh century before Christ. Roman inscriptions, however, with the exception of a very fragmentary text from the sixth century recorded on the *lapis niger* in the Roman Forum, do not begin to appear until around 300 B.C. By then, of course, the change had already been effected. Therefore, in order to be accurate, the sound-law under discusssion has since been altered to read: "Proto-Indo-European [s] in intervocalic position became intervocalic [r] in *Early* Latin."

Of course, not all the exceptions could be explained. But even so, the neogrammarians upheld their fundamental postulate that sound-laws are without exception. All aberrances, they maintained, are due simply to our ignorance or imperfect knowledge of linguistic history, as borne out by the countless times that "exceptions" had ceased to exist once adequate information was available. Just as scholars employ the comparative method *as if* it were wholly accurate, so did the neogrammarians prefer to say that sound-laws are utterly valid, choosing to let the exceptions stand, awaiting the day when new knowledge would solve the problem. We of today, although accepting the principle of regularity of sound-change, should prefer a somewhat less dramatic and more carefully formulated statement than Leskien's highly figurative "Sound-laws have no exception." A more acceptable phrasing might be: "Within certain limits of time and space, the same sounds, given the same conditions, behave in the same way."

The strength of the neogrammarian approach is its insistence upon methodological rigor and its determination to deal only with the physical phenomena of language. But this very objectivity came in for severe criticism. One of the principal charges leveled against the new method was that it was atomistic in its approach to knowledge, and that this preoccupation with isolated features of language caused its practitioners to stress form rather than function, tending thereby to make of linguistics a barren, purely descriptive process that was essentially non-intellectual and hence unworthy of scholarly attention.

When we recall the unbridled speculations and wild flights of fancy that characterized earlier epochs of linguistic investigation, it is difficult to understand why serious students should have resisted these efforts to introduce a disciplined and controllable methodology. Some of their objections stemmed we know from personal animosities. More general, however, was the suspicion that the neogrammarians were trying to "dehumanize" language—that they were trying to deny to the human intellect its creative control over speech. The new theory seemed to imply that language had a sort of independent existence, and that it was governed by mechanistic forces beyond the power of human direction. Understandably, a doctrine of this sort was most unpalatable to scholars trained in the philosophical tradition of the West, for whom grammar had always been a handmaid of logic: *philosophus grammaticam invenit!*

It is therefore not surprising that the neogrammarian movement met with considerable opposition in Europe—especially outside its homeland, Germany. In the United States, however, largely because of a generation of German-trained philologists in our universities, the neogrammarian tradition is still very strong. Indeed, it is probably not incorrect to say that a neogrammarian orientation is more noticeable among our own linguists than among the scholars of contemporary Germany. This statement will be dealt with in greater detail in the next chapter, when we discuss the contributions of the late Leonard Bloomfield to American linguistics.

But to return to our historical survey. In the closing years of the nineteenth century both the theory and the methods of historico-comparative linguistics were given definitive treatment. In 1880, for example, there appeared the first edition of Hermann Paul's *Principles of Linguistic History (Prinzipien der Sprachgeschichte)*, the most thorough study of linguistic change we possess. Because Paul's attempts to explain these changes occasionally bog down in a morass of psychologizing, his work has suffered an unfortunate eclipse—unfortunate because nowhere else will the student find such a wealth of examples illustrating all varieties of linguistic change: phonetic, analogic, and semantic. The fifth edition of 1920 should be given preference.

In 1886 there began appearing what is probably the most impressive achievement of comparative linguistic scholarship: the monumental *Comparative Indo-European Grammar* (*Grundriss der vergleichenden Grammatik der indogermanischen Sprachen*) by Karl Brugmann and Berthold Delbrück. The second edition of this massive work, published over the years 1897–1916, is still quoted today. Later studies have disclosed errors in it; many of the suggested etymologies and roots are only guesses—probably incorrect—but the vast scope of the project, plus the wealth of examples cited, assures its continued use for many years to come. It should be emphasized, however, that contemporary scholarship has wrought many changes in Brugmann's reconstructions.

Mention must also be made of another and more recent grammar of Indo-European: Hermann Hirt's *Indogermanische Grammatik* (Heidelberg, 1921–37) in seven volumes. Because of certain theories and premises, however, Hirt's work has met with much resistance both here and abroad, although it has nevertheless exerted considerable influence.

The most able expositor and stylist of this era was the Sorbonne professor, Antoine Meillet, whose *Introduction to the Comparative Study of Indo-European* (*Introduction à l'étude comparative des langues indo-européennes*) is still the classic text in this field. The reader should use the third edition of 1912. Meillet wrote lucidly and brilliantly on many phases of Indo-European comparative linguistics.

Although a discussion of current trends in comparative linguistics is beyond the scope of this book, the student should realize that it is still a vigorous and productive area of scholarship. Indeed, Indo-European comparative studies are presently enjoying something of a renaissance in the United States. Admittedly the most difficult of the linguistic disciplines in which to achieve competency —requiring a good background in Latin, Greek, and Sanskrit, plus a specialist's command of at least one *family* of the Indo-European languages—it offers a high degree of intellectual satisfaction to the serious student with a taste for humanistic learning and a flair for languages.

It should be mentioned at least in passing that the methods of comparison and reconstruction perfected by the Indo-Europeanists are being used with telling success by specialists in the languages of certain aboriginal societies. Edward Sapir, for instance, was able to demonstrate quite convincingly the northern origins of the southern Athabaskan tribes (Apache and Navaho) of North American Indians, and Leonard Bloomfield's reconstruction of Proto-Algonquian is even today considered a classic example of brilliant technique enhanced by spectacular results. (Certain of Bloomfield's reconstructions were confirmed by the later discovery of another Algonquian dialect which had preserved some of the features no longer present in the languages first investigated.)

More recently, Isidore Dyen of Yale has been engaged in the classification of the Malayo-Polynesian languages, an extremely complex and diverse linguistic group encompassing perhaps as many as five hundred languages. A similar project is being conducted for the indigenous languages of Africa by Joseph Greenberg of Columbia University. The comparative method of establishing linguistic relationships is the basic tool of all such studies.

Most of the more dramatic chapters in the recent history of the discipline—one is immediately reminded of the current status of the laryngeal theory—cannot be reviewed satisfactorily in a few pages within a text designed for the non-specialist. Nevertheless, I should like to attempt a discussion of one late development that has caught the fancy of layman and specialist alike, probably because it has suggested an analogy with atomic behavior. I refer to the still highly controversial subject known as "lexicostatistics."

One of the most annoying weaknesses of the comparative method is that it cannot with any accuracy date the linguistic changes that it reveals; it can establish only a "before and after" relationship. Its chronology is relative rather than absolute, or, to use the terminology of statistics, the comparative method is capable of "topological" dating but not of "metric" dating. We know, for instance, that German and English are descended from a common linguistic prototype, but we cannot accurately determine when the "split" occurred: we cannot really tell how old English or German is.

Early in the 1950's the American anthropologist and linguist, Morris Swadesh (1909——), devised a procedure for the metrical dating of linguistic relationships, a procedure known as lexico-statistical dating or glottochronology, considered by some to be the most significant development in historico-comparative linguistics since the formulation of the comparative method itself. The method derives in principle from chemistry, where it was earlier discovered that by determining the amount of radioactivity still remaining in certain carbon compounds, one could measure the age of organic substances.

Although the element carbon (atomic weight 12) is not radio-active, one of its isotopes does possess this property. This isotope, carbon-14, created by the constant bombardment of cosmic rays in the upper atmosphere on nitrogen-14 atoms, unites with oxygen to form a variety of carbon dioxide, which is present in fixed propor-tions in normal carbon dioxide (CO_2). Since one of the products of oxidation is carbon dioxide, carbon-14 is therefore a constant factor in all organic metabolism. Willard F. Libby, for many years at the Institute for Nuclear Studies at the University of Chicago but now a professor of chemistry at the University of California, Los Angeles, demonstrated that all organic substances contain a pro-portion of about one-trillionth of a gram of carbon-14 to one gram of carbon-12. With the death of the cellular organism the consump-tion of carbon-14 of course ceases, but the amount absorbed into the body during life remains and slowly disintegrates at a constant rate. By determining the amount of radioactive carbon still remain-ing in an organic substance, it therefore becomes possible to deter-mine its "age," that is, when the process of oxidation ceased; or, otherwise stated, when it died. Professor Libby received the Nobel Prize in chemistry in 1960 for this discovery.

The reliability of this procedure depends again upon our knowl-edge of the "life expectancy" of radioactive atoms. Physicists have worked out the transformation series of many elements, and have accurately determined how long it takes metrically for a given element to become inert, that is, to disintegrate. A given mass of radium, for example, will lose one-half its mass in 1,690 years, but will not lose the other half in the next 1,690 years. During the second period it will lose half of the amount remaining at the end of the first period, leaving one-fourth of the total at the end of 3,380 years. During the next 1,690 years the one-fourth will dwindle to one-eighth, and so on. This is the explanation of the term "half-life" of an element.

The application of this knowledge to anthropology or archeology is fairly apparent. If some organic material such as wood, charcoal, or cloth gives off a certain measurable amount of radiation, its age can be determined by referring to the "life expectancy" table of the radioactive form of carbon, the isotope carbon-14, which has a half-life of 5,100 years. Within a time-depth ranging from about one thousand to twenty thousand years, this method yields results reliable to within 5 to 10 per cent. The accuracy of this technique has been tested on material which can be dated otherwise. Of immediate interest to students of language, this procedure has been used to help date the Dead Sea scrolls.

Returning now to Professor Swadesh's contribution, he developed a method for determining the "life expectancy" of a *word*. The results of his efforts are most interesting.

Working from languages for which there are historical records, he constructed a word-list of 200 items (later reduced to 100) which he considered minimally bound to any one culture. These words served as a core vocabulary. When applied to languages which the comparative method had shown to be related, it was determined that the rate of word-loss was remarkably constant for all languages investigated. In terms of percentage, a given language will preserve 81 per cent of the core vocabulary after the first thousand years of separation from the common antecedent. After another millennium it will have preserved 81 per cent of the first 81 per cent, and so on—similar to the radium example. Or, working back from the present, if we find that two languages have 66 per cent of the basic vocabulary in common, we assume them to have been separated for 1,000 years; that is, each language has diverged for 1,000 years (=81 per cent) from the point of their separation. If 44 per cent is cognate, then we assume 2,000 years of separation, and so forth. In other words, lexicostatistics gives us a method for assigning an approximate calendar year to the time when a given language split off from its proto-stock and began an independent existence.

The value of this procedure as a research tool is still questioned (or even denied) by many workers, not only because it is very difficult to construct a vocabulary core that is both cognate and non-cultural, but also because the results of such studies sometimes apparently contradict extra-linguistic evidence of a convincing and usually reliable nature. For instance, the validity of the mathematical formulations by which the data are processed and evaluated has recently been impugned. However, even if the formulas have to be revised, more immediately important than the theory's ability to assign absolute metric values is its practical usefulness as an approximate yardstick for establishing relative genetic proximity of languages within a proven genetic family. Lexicostatistics is, in any event, an extremely interesting development, and—if its mathematical premises can be agreed upon—may yet prove to be all it purports to be: a powerful and reliable technique not only for establishing lines of linguistic proximity, but also for determining the metrical age of languages.

THE TWENTIETH CENTURY TO 1950

If the nineteenth century was the Golden Age of historico-comparative linguistics, then the twentieth may properly be called the age of descriptive linguistics—"descriptive" in the sense of Wilhelm von Humboldt's definition of the term: "The analysis of language as an internally articulated organism." This approach to language is today known as "structural linguistics"; the purpose of this chapter will be to trace the origins of structuralism, and to examine a few of its basic tenets as formulated or modified by certain scholars, who—perhaps more than any others—gave direction and definition to the movement.

The greatest theoretician of the new era, and the one who first elaborated the structural principle into a well-defined theory, was the eminent Swiss comparativist, Ferdinand de Saussure (1857–1913). His lectures were collected, edited, and published after his death by two of his students, themselves prominent scholars (Charles Bally and Albert Sechehaye), under the title *Cours de linguistique générale*. Published in 1916, this text has only recently appeared in an English translation by Wade Baskin with the title *Course in General Linguistics* (New York: Philosophical Library, 1959). All quotations are from the English version.

Saussure's great service to the study of language lies in a series of rigorous distinctions and definitions which he made concerning the nature of language. He first of all tried to make clear to himself just what is meant by the term "language." As a preliminary step toward this definition he attempted to describe the speech act. In his own words:

> Suppose that two people, A and B, are conversing with each other: Suppose that the opening of the circuit is in A's brain, where mental facts (concepts) are associated with representations of the linguistic sounds (sound-

61

images) that are used for their expression. A given concept unlocks a corresponding sound-image in the brain;
this purely *psychological* phenomenon is followed in turn
by a physiological process: the brain transmits an impulse
corresponding to the image to the organs used in produc-
ing sounds. Then the sound waves travel from the mouth
of A to the ear of D. a purely physical process. Next, the
circuit continues in B, but the order is reversed: from the
ear to the brain, the physiological transmission of the
sound-image; in the brain, the psychological association of
the image with the corresponding concept [*Course*, pp.
11–12].

Certain facts about the nature of language are at once obvious
from this description. For instance, are concepts the stuff of language? No, because a concept is non-verbal, purely psychological.
Actually, the only phase of the process which is directly perceptible
is the spoken part. But is this necessarily language? No, for it can
be just noise: indiscriminate vocalizing or babbling. Before a sound
can have meaning it must be *related* to a concept, and it is precisely
this relationship that Saussure defines as the essence of language.
Language serves as a link between thought and sound.

As is obvious from this statement, Saussure conceived of this
union between concept and expression ("signified" and "signifier"
in his terminology) as a *function* rather than a *thing*. What emerges
as a linguistic entity is a form that has meaning only to the extent
that it unites a sound and a concept, and this entity resulting from
the association of the signifier with the signified he calls the
"linguistic sign."

Since linguistics to Saussure is properly the study of this "sign,"
we should understand something about its nature. First of all, he
considered it to be *arbitrary*. He uses this term in the Aristotelian
sense: the sign is arbitrary in that it is unmotivated; there is no
inner relationship to the sequence of sounds that serves as the
signifier. Oddly enough, it is precisely this arbitrariness of the

"word" (since this is the audible, perceptible part of the sign) that tends to make it immutable, not subject to change. Although we deny any necessary correlation between word and thing, we have nevertheless a vocabulary. It is therefore rather pointless to argue about the rational relationship between signifier and the signified. On what basis would we propose a change? Is there any reason why we should not want to refer to the luminary center of our planetary system as the "sun"? Thus, reasons Saussure, the sign tends to be *immutable*. There are of course other factors that work to inhibit linguistic change: the vastness of our total vocabulary, the complex structure of language—which is understood only after much study —and the peculiar inertia of language; it is everybody's property, and the efforts of the few will not overcome the drag of the many. Most important of all, perhaps, is that language has its roots forever firmly in the past. We have received it from our ancestors, and there is little we can do—or want to do!—other than to accept it. "Because the sign is arbitrary, it follows no law other than that of tradition, and because it is based on tradition, it is arbitrary" (*Course*, p. 74).

And yet words *do* change—both in form and meaning. Why? Because, says Saussure, the "bond" between the signified and the signifier has somehow become relaxed or displaced. In older German, for instance, the word for "one-third" was *dritteil* (that is, *drit-teil:* "third-part"); in modern German this word has become *Drittel*. Although the concept has remained unchanged, there has been a shift in relationship. *Drittel* not only has a different phonetic form, but it has shifted completely away from the noun *Teil* "part." It is now a different word. Or, to use another term basic to Saussure's system, the shift in relationship between the signifier and the signified has changed the "value" of the linguistic sign.

He makes an important distinction between the naming of a concept and the value that such a name or "signification" has in a language. Whereas the former process relates a single concept immediately to a single sound-image, its "value" is determined by its relationship within the total vocabulary in a language. For example, the word for "sheep" in Spanish is *carnero,* in French, *mouton.* These three words all have the same signification but not the same value, since English *sheep* refers to the live animal, whereas mutton is used to denote the cooked meat. This distinction does not exist in Spanish or French. Inasmuch as English has two terms for the animal—*sheep* and *mutton*—the Spanish and French words, though having the same signification as English *sheep,* have a different value.

Saussure applied his principle of values not only to the conceptual but also to the material aspects of language. Just as the conceptual value of the sign is determined by its relation to all the other signs in the language (that is, by its environment), so are the sounds characterized, "not, as one might think, by their own positive quality but simply by the fact that they are distinct. Phonemes are above all else opposing, relative, and negative entities" (*Course,* p. 119). Language, according to Saussure, is simply the functioning of linguistic oppositions; these oppositions yield a pattern of relationships—a *Gestalt*—the study of which constitutes linguistics.

Another distinction which he found useful in trying to define the subject matter of linguistics was that between *parole* (utterance) and *langue* (language).

Language leads a dual existence. There is first of all the flow of living speech. This is personalized language—your speech and my speech. This aspect of language, to which Saussure gave the name *parole,* is a physical reality that varies from person to person. But there is also another aspect of language (*le langage*) which he called *langue;* it is to this that we refer when we speak of the English language, the German language, and so on. *Langue* is an abstract linguistic system existing quite apart from the individual. It is constant, supra-individualistic, and generalized; the individual speaker can neither create it nor modify it (with certain rare exceptions). A *langue* is not spoken by anybody, but is a composite body of linguistic phenomena derived as it were from the personal dialects (*paroles*) of all native speakers. It is in essence a social phenomenon, having reality only as a social institution. For this reason *langue* is always and only contemporary to the society with which it is identified.

The last sentence could be rephrased to state that a *langue* has an existence limited *in time* to the society of which it is a part. Since language constitutes a system of values, insisted Saussure, it obviously can only be studied within the framework of that society which determines those values. This led him to distinguish sharply between the study of "static" (synchronic) and "evolutionary" (diachronic) linguistics. In order to describe the former he speaks of an axis of simultaneous events, whereas the latter is referred to as an axis of successive events. Synchronic linguistics is the study of linguistic events on the same time level, while diachronic studies are concerned with linguistic events through successive layers of time. The one is descriptive, the other is historical. It is a major tenet of Saussure's teaching that investigations on these two distinct and different linguistic planes are not amenable to the same methods of research, and that the boundaries of each study should always be clearly delineated.

The study of phonetic change, for example, he reckoned to the diachronic plane. Sound-changes are historical events that take place quite without intention on the part of the generations of speakers involved. Each generation uses the same general sound-pattern and no one perceives that certain classes of sounds are "drifting" away from a previous norm. Old English *stān* has become New English *stone*, and yet the shift was so gradual that no generation was aware that it was changing anything. The "state" of a language at any particular time, therefore, is fortuitous. Synchronic events, on the other hand, are always significant and indicate a conscious selection between two or more structural or lexical possibilities (a change of value).

As an example: In Old High German the plural form of the word *gast* "guest" was at one time something like **gasti*. At a later stage in the language, low back vowels became palatalized or "fronted" when followed in the next syllable by a high front vowel. In this way **gasti* became *gesti*. Then, because the primary stress fell on the root syllable, the final *i*-vowel was "weakened" to the phonetic equivalent of orthographic *e*, resulting eventually in *geste* (the modern spelling is *Gäste*). It is important to bear in mind that the diachronic change of *a* to *e* under the influence of a following *i* had— *at the time it happened*—nothing to do with selecting a new marker for indicating the plural of substantives; the plural-marker at that time was still final *-i*. Each generation of speakers quite by chance took advantage of an existing phonetic distinction and let it signal the difference between singular and plural. On the synchronic level, however, the conscious selection of either **gasti* or *gesti* as a plural always involved the contrasting form of the singular, *gast;* the selection was conscious and deliberate. Of significance is the observation that diachronic phenomena, though independent of structural systems, may certainly modify them.

Saussure's influence upon subsequent linguistic theory has understandably been of major importance. Indeed, in the Western world at any rate, all hues of structuralism have come under his influence. His studies of values, for example, were later expanded into techniques for determining not only the limits that set off a given signification, but, equally productive, for structuring the entire vocabulary into *semantic* units. He carefully distinguished between two types of value-relationship: one based upon the linear sequence of linguistic terms as they occur in the speech-act, the other derived from the semantic associations that serve to arrange words into cognate groups. Combinations based upon linearity he calls "syntagms"; these have their origin and value solely in discourse, in articulated speech. The semantic relationship, on the other hand, is strictly speaking not linguistic but psychological, its value being dependent upon mental co-ordinations. This type of relationship Saussure termed "associative."

Since these "associative relations" are not based upon any observable, describable feature of arrangement *in speech*, many workers in the United States would not call this sort of study "linguistic"; they would ascribe it to semantics or perhaps to psychology. I dwell upon it here, however, because we are attempting in this chapter to trace the origin and development of the structural principle: the cardinal contribution of the twentieth century to the study of language. This notion of structure as applied to vocabulary has resulted in some significant advances in a field which, though possibly not "linguistic" by close definition, is nevertheless of considerable interest to students of language. I refer to what is generally called "linguistic field-theory."

This theory derives from another idea—first proposed in print by the German philosopher-linguist Wilhelm von Humboldt (1767–1835)—that "man lives with the world about him principally, indeed . . . exclusively, as language presents it to him." Humboldt buttressed this assertion with another statement, equally daring, that language is not a *thing*, but an *activity:* the active, formative force of the intellect. In order to understand a culture, therefore, it was first necessary to determine how the living power of the word had shaped a people's construct of the world about them.

Humboldt did not propose a technique for doing this, but his ideas lived on and bore fruit. Saussure's belief that language is a *function* and not a *form* most likely derives either directly or indirectly from Humboldt's writings—probably from his celebrated work on the nature of linguistic structure and its effect upon the intellectual development of the human race (*Über die Verschiedenheit des menschlichen Sprachbaues und ihren Einfluss auf die geistige Entwicklung des Menschengeschlechts*, 1836). It was Saussure, however, who proposed a method for investigating function, namely, that of patterning or structuring, and in this way plotting the activity that *is* language in its recognizable and describable relationships. As we have seen, he wanted to study the connection not only of forms but also of concepts. This latter notion, coupled as it is to Humboldtian philosophy, has received the attention of a group of scholars—most of them Germans (Walter Porzig, Jost Trier, Leo Weisgerber)—who have elaborated the notion of concept-patterning and developed certain techniques for establishing the "linguistic field"—hence the term "field-theory."

Of special interest to American students is a comparison between field-theory in Europe and some similar theories proposed by the late Benjamin Lee Whorf (1897–1941) in the United States. Most students of language in America are now familiar with certain of Whorf's writings, readily available in the edition by John B. Carroll: *Language, Thought, and Reality* (New York, 1956). His hypothesis, apparently independently arrived at, that a people's view of reality is in large part determined by the linguistic mold into which they are cast ("linguistic relativity"), and his examples drawn from certain American Indian languages, have quickened the interest of many linguists, even though one must add that he has made few outright converts. The "field-theory" point of view, however, in its implications and practice, in its European as well as its American garb, is an interesting extension of the structural principle to the conceptual level.

Another linguistic movement that took its inspiration in part from Saussure's *Cours de linguistique générale* is that which began with what is known either as the "Prague School" or the "Prague Circle" (the original organization was called *le cercle linguistique de Prague*). The name of the scholar most influential in giving direction to the movement is Nikolas S. Trubetzkoy (1890–1938), although Professor Roman Jakobson (1896———)—now of Harvard—has probably been most responsible for extending Prague School theory and practice into new areas of research. For the sake of historical perspective, however, the student may be interested in a brief restatement of some of the basic ideas of *early* Prague School "phonology" (phonemics), although he must realize that since that time the techniques of analysis have undergone constant refinement; likewise the terminology has been subjected in part to redefinition or modification. The most complete and authoritative statement of principles and methods as originally formulated is contained in Prince Trubetzkoy's *Principles of Phonology* (*Grundzüge der Phonologie* [Prague, 1939]; there is also a French version: *Principes de phonologie* [Paris, 1949]).

Founders of the Prague School called their particular approach to the study of language "phonology," which they defined as the study of the *function* of speech-sounds, and because of this emphasis they are sometimes referred to as "functionalists." Although fully conversant with the theories and methods of the leading European linguists, they were primarily indebted to certain Slavic scholars for background, training, and inspiration. Trubetzkoy, for instance, points out that a professor at the University of Moscow, J. Baudouin de Courtenay (Polish by birth), recognized as early as 1870 the necessity of distinguishing between the sounds of a language and the manner in which those sounds were used to structure a given language. The techniques for determining the *Sprachgebilde* of a language—the way it structures its sound-units into specific patterns—are nevertheless the unique and important contribution of the Prague School to modern linguistic science.

Basic to their method of sound-structuring is the use of contrast or opposition, for only by establishing differences did they believe it possible to construct a system of interrelationships. Their criterion for determining which sounds are significantly contrastive is meaning; phonetic differences that do not signal semantic differences are not distinctive—are not "phonemic" (or "phonematic" as they would say). Indeed, that which serves to differentiate the phonological unit—the *phoneme*—is actually not the sound itself, but rather the sound's contrastive function. A phoneme, therefore, may be defined as the sum of these differentiating functions. It is not a thing, but an abstraction. Sounds in themselves are not phonemes; they are phonemes only insofar as they serve to distinguish meaning. Those sounds in a language which function phonemically—that is, significantly—are determined simply by contrasting two sounds in identical environments. If this contrast is accompanied by a difference in meaning, then the phonetic contrast is also phonemic; that which is relevant or meaningful about a sound is this contrastive function. Because the essence of the phoneme centers on this principle of contrast, Trubetzkoy developed an elaborate set of contrast criteria for identifying and classifying what he called "phonological oppositions." We might mention a few of them.

There is nothing absolute about a phoneme. Any significant feature of sound—as sound—is only *relatively* different from other significant features of sound. Some pairs will have much more in common—will share a greater number of phonetic characteristics— than other pairs. Because this sort of information is fundamental to a complete statement of phonemic patterning, Trubetzkoy sets up a type of opposition which he calls "bilateral." German /k/ and /χ/ (slashes are used to indicate phonemic notation) may serve as an example: The features which they have in common—oral, velar, voiceless—do not occur simultaneously in any other phoneme of Standard German, thereby permitting the obvious remark that these two phonemes are "closely related." A "multilateral opposition," on the other hand, is a much more loosely established relationship: /a/ and /i/, for instance, are alike only to the extent that both are vowels, a quality shared by any other pair of vowels.

Other phonological oppositions may be "proportional" or "isolated." They are proportional if the same contrastive feature also serves as the differentiating criterion for other pairs of phonemes. For example, sonority is the contrastive feature between not only /p/ and /b/, but also between /t/ and /d/, and /k/ and /g/. An example of isolated opposition is that between Spanish /r/ and /r̄/: duration of the trill is *not* a contrastive feature of any other pair of phonemes in the language.

Or an opposition may be described as "privative," that is, one member of a contrastive pair may be characterized by the presence of a certain feature, the other by its absence: aspiration–lack of of aspiration; nasalization–lack of nasalization, and so forth.

Another type of opposition occurs when two sounds contrast in some positions but not in others. Spanish /r/ and /r̄/, for instance, contrast only intervocalically; English /p/ and /b/ do not contrast after /s/. This function of lack of contrast in specific positions Trubetzkoy calls "neutralization" (*Aufhebung* in the German text). In non-contrastive position either of the phonemes of the bilateral opposition (or a non-distinctive variant) will occur, but the distribution will be automatically regulated by the structure of the language. In Spanish, as a case in point, although /r/ and /r̄/ contrast intervocalically (*pero–perro*)—and must therefore be treated as separate phonemes—/r̄/ occurs otherwise only initially, whereas /r/ is limited to final position and to certain medial consonantal clusters. This neutralized or environmentally determined variant is given a special name: the *archiphoneme*.

The final step in phonemic patterning is to chart the functional relations between the contrasts that have been established. This structuring of the oppositions—as we shall learn a bit later—is especially important in studying the historical development of a language, for it provides us with some most interesting insights into why certain phonetic changes took place.

That phonetic feature which unites two phonemes into a contrastive pair, Trubetzkoy describes as "correlative"; and in turn he defines a "correlation" as a binary contrast shared by more than one correlated pair: thus, /p/–/b/, /t/–/d/, /k/–/g/ constitute a correlation of sonority. Phonemes, however, are capable of sharing in more than one correlation. In Sanskrit, for example, the stops constitute simultaneously one correlation based upon sonority, and another based upon aspiration. These two functions yield the following pattern of correlations:

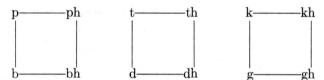

Such a pattern or combination of phonemes of the same order (that is, of the same place of articulation) that in turn share other features of articulation—in the above case sonority and aspiration—the Prague structuralists refer to as a "bundle of correlations."

If we were to sum up what Trubetzkoy teaches about the nature of the phoneme, we might risk the following statement: The phoneme is a bundle of simultaneous distinctive features consisting of binary contrasts or oppositions, being simply the sum of these binary contrasts, and having validity only in a given *and relative* set of phonetic contrasts.

Saussure, it will be remembered, had made the pronouncement that descriptive and historical studies are not amenable to the same methods—that they are in fact methodologically incompatible. Consistency more or less forced him to this conclusion, because his method of determining the semantic relationships that account for the structuring of the social phenomenon he called *langue* was of course not applicable to historical investigations tracing the development of individual sounds. This sort of diachronic study he called "phonetics," and to him it meant simply recording the sound-changes that a language had undergone (as reflected in documents, of course), but with little attempt to determine causes. Obviously, his socially oriented approach tended to minimize the importance and significance of the historical study of language.

The first open break with the Saussurian tenet that diachronic and synchronic studies must be mutually exclusive came in 1928, when Trubetzkoy, Jakobson, and Karcevskij presented a manifesto to the First International Congress of Linguists at The Hague, a manifesto in which they maintained that phonological methods are theoretically just as applicable to diachronic as to synchronic studies—that the scholar can in fact pass back and forth on the temporal axes without jeopardizing the validity of either his procedures or his results. These were bold words—and yet fruitful, because it is precisely in the area of diachronic linguistics that Prague School theory and practice seems to many to have made its most distinctive contribution to the study of language. The scholar whose name is perhaps most closely associated with present-day diachronic linguistic research is Professor André Martinet of the Sorbonne.

The following paragraphs will attempt to set forth in broad out-

line certain of the principal features of diachronic phonology or diachronic phonemics (the terms are here used synonymously).

Diachronic phonemics is interested in sound-change only to the
extent that it has brought about alterations in the structure of a
language, for only in such cases can one say that a given change was
"functional"—was "significant." These functional or purposeful
types of phonetic change, as opposed to those changes which did
not result in systemic modifications, are called "phonological transformations." Functional change, moreover, since it involves a restructuring of the *meaningful* elements of a language, is by definition a conscious and intellectualized act; not, as simple phonetic
change, an unconscious, evolutionary development that may extend in time across several generations of speakers. As a word of
caution, however, it might be stressed that all functional change
finds its origin in phonetic change.

The concept of functional change presupposes a system, and—of
considerable importance to the study of language—these systems
seem to observe a definite and demonstrable type of *harmony* and
economy, with the result that phonemic oppositions that are unique,
isolated, or asymmetrical in structure, that is, that do not conform
to a prevailing correlation, tend to be eliminated (but not necessarily are). One of the functionally most significant things about a correlation is that it evinces the economy with which a given linguistic
system structures its phonemes: the greater the number of correlations, the greater the structural economy of a language; for then
it will have differentiated the maximum number of phonemes by
means of the minimum number of distinctive phonetic features.

As an illustration of how function may affect structure, let us
suppose that in a given language we have an order of sounds, joined
together by correlations depending upon points of articulation
(localization) and upon sonority versus non-sonority (voiced–
voiceless). Let us further assume that this language has bilabial,
dental, and velar voiceless stops, but that their voiced counterparts
are limited to only two of the three positions: bilabial and dental.
We could chart this situation as follows:

k–

p–b   t–d

The principles of linguistic economy and harmony would tend to resolve this uneven distribution in one of three ways. Total correlation could be achieved by the development of a voiced velar stop, thus filling the empty space in the pattern (k–g). Another possibility is that the correlation of localization might win out, resulting in a simplified pattern:

k

p   t

Or the correlation of sonority could triumph, thus reducing the scheme to:

p–b   t–d

Prague School adherents claim that many structural changes in the historical development of a language can be explained by determining the phonetic functions that fashion the pattern of correlation.

Some oppositions occur with greater frequency than others. This observation has led to another definition that has proved of value to the diachronic study of language. In English—as an illustration —the /p/–/b/ opposition is said to have a high "functional yield," because there are many pairs of otherwise homonymous words distinguished solely by the contrastive features between these two phonemes. Conversely, the yield in English of the contrastive pair /θ/–/ð/ is low, since this particular feature of correlation serves to distinguish few word-pairs (*thigh–thy; mouth–mouthe,* and a few others). It is a principle of diachronic phonemics that a phoneme of low functional yield tends to disappear, resulting in a modification of the linguistic structure. Here again, though, the importance of a functional analysis of the phonemic system is borne out, for if (as is true of English) a particular binarism, say that of sonority between the pair /p/–/b/, is itself part of a correlation that binds together an *order* of correlated pairs (/p/–/b/, /t/–/d/, /k/–/g/), then, even though the functional yield of one of the binarisms is low, it will tend to be preserved in the language.

As stated earlier, diachronic phonemics is interested primarily in determining which phonetic changes became functional changes: which ones can be classified as "transformations." It has accordingly devised several definitions and techniques for determining the functional significance of the many types of sound-change that characterize the growth and development of language. Basic to all of them, however, is the distinction between a phonemic and a non-phonemic change in sound. The reader should be clear on this point.

For instance, some scholars hold that eighteenth-century English had pure long vowels of the sort [i:, e:, u:, o:] that occurred in such words as *geese, eight, goose,* and *goat.* Some time later these vowels—according to this theory—were diphthongized, resulting in the types that we normally use today in pronouncing the spellings just given, so that phonetically we should now have to record the sounds as [ij, ej, uw, ow]. This sort of change—if it actually took place—is of no *functional* importance; the phonetic criteria of the phonemes have indeed been modified, but the phonemic *structure* of the language has remained constant.

But let us consider the effects of the Great Vowel Shift of Middle English as an example of a sound-change that brought with it a change in structure—a functional change. I quote from pages 284–85 of Otto Jespersen's *Language, Its Nature, Development and Origin* (New York: Macmillan Co., 1922):

Middle English	Elizabethan	Modern English
(1) bite [bi:tə]	[beit]	[bait] bite
(2) bete [be:tə]	[bi:t]	[bi:t] beet
(3) bete [bɛ:tə]	[be:t]	[bi:t] beat
(4) abate [abá:tə]	[əbæ:t]	[əbéit] abate

When the sound of (2) was raised into [i:], the sound of (1) had already left that position and had been diphthongized, and when the sound of (3) was raised from an open into a close *e*, (2) had already become [iː]; (4) could not become [æː] or [ɛː] till (3) had become a comparatively close *e* sound. The four vowels, as it were, climbed the ladder without ever reaching each other—a climbing which took centuries and in each case implied intermediate steps not indicated in our survey. No clashings could occur so long as each category kept its distance from the sounds above and below, and thus we find the Elizabethans as scrupulously as Chaucer kept the four classes of words apart in their rimes. But in the seventeenth century class (3) was raised, and as no corresponding change had taken place with (2), the two classes have now fallen together with the single sound [iː]. This entails a certain number of homophones such as had not been created through the preceding equidistant changes.

Another well-known instance of sound-change with accompanying structural change is found in Spanish. This change resulted not only in fewer phonemes, but also in the appearance of a new phoneme.

The early language had a voiceless and voiced pre-palatal spirant—[š] and [ž]—so that the spellings *dixo* "he said," *hijo* "son," and *coger* "to catch," were pronounced [díːšoː], [híːžo], and [koːžéːr], respectively. By the beginning of the seventeenth century these two phonemes had merged into one: a voiceless velar spirant [χ], a sound, incidentally, that had been lacking in the phonemic inventory of medieval Spanish.

This change had two effects on the structure of the language: one, since Castilian already had the voiceless velar stop [k], the development of a corresponding spirant permitted a new contrast. This—coupled with the disappearance of the pre-palatal pair—resulted in a restructuring of the phonemic system. Second, the new pair was differentiated by the same feature that contrasted /p/–/f/ and /t/–/θ/, thus setting up a new (or at least expanded) system of correlations.

As an example of diachronic structural methods applied to a somewhat larger problem, let us take up again the now familiar Germanic Consonant Shift. One of the most intriguing attempts in recent years to determine the causes underlying both this and the High German Shift is that of Jean Fourquet as set forth in his monograph, *The Germanic Consonant Shifts* (*Les mutations consonantiques du germanique*, 2d ed.; Paris, 1956). Incidentally, he considers the High German Shift to be but another and later phase of the Germanic, using the terms "first" and "second" mutation to distinguish between them.

To Fourquet the change of the individual, discrete sound is not of the essence: to say that Indo-European [p] becomes Germanic [f] is a true enough statement, but it misses the point. Even a statement that the voiceless stops become in Germanic the corresponding voiceless spirants is not adequate. The only meaningful statement is one that relates *form* to *function*—one that reveals the factors which *caused* the repatterning of the phonemes. The linguistically meaningful fact, therefore, is that because of a change in correlation, a realignment of the phonemic structure has taken place. Approached from this point of view, the Germanic Shift (and we shall limit ourselves for purposes of this demonstration to it) takes on quite a different perspective. In order to appreciate this, let us first give this shift in tabular form as it usually appears in the conventional (neogrammarian) handbooks:

GERMANIC CONSONANT SHIFT

Indo-European	Germanic
p, t, k, kʷ	f, þ, χ, χʷ
bh, dh, gh, gʷh	(via β, ð, γ, γʷ) b, d, g, gw
b, d, g, gʷ	p, t, k, kw

NOTE: The use of *h* in the digraphs above indicates aspiration.

For purposes of comparison, bear in mind that this sort of summation stresses the fate of the *individual* sounds, even though—for the sake of convenience—they are listed in phonetic series.

Fourquet's presentation of the same phenomena, but arranged structurally, is represented by Figure 2.

Frame 1 structures the consonants of Indo-European prior to the beginnings of any of the changes that resulted in the emergence of Germanic as a separate linguistic entity. Fourquet assumes that already in late Indo-European (or, for our purposes, Pre-Germanic), a dialect area including Germanic became characterized by a marked increase in aspiration, which resulted—so he feels—from a weakening of articulation. This relaxation of muscular tone or tautness—for whatever psychological or neurophysiological reasons —caused the previously unaspirated voiceless stops to become

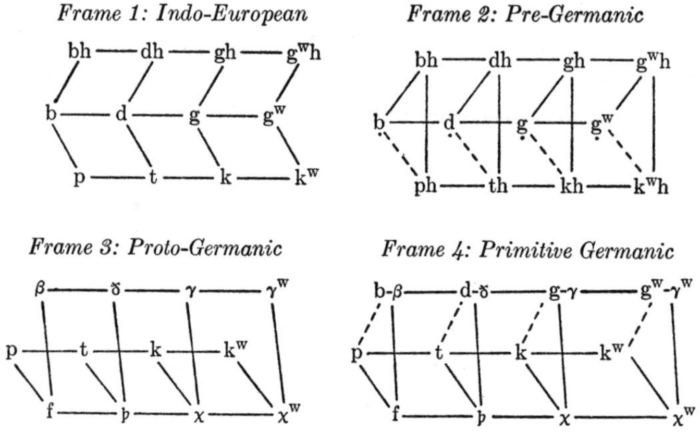

Fig. 2

aspirated, and the previously voiced series to take on a characteristic lenis quality—indicated by a dot under the symbols in question (see Fig. 2, Frame 2). Notice that the phonetic feature of increased aspiration has brought with it certain "phonological" changes; that is, a different set of correlations. At this stage there is a correlation of *sonority* binding together the voiceless and voiced aspirated stops, and a correlation of *aspiration* uniting the unaspirated lenis voiced stops and the aspirated voiced stops. If, because of extreme lenition, the unaspirated voiced stops became voiceless (as they eventually did), then the correlation is reversed, as shown by the broken line.

This weakening of articulation—which characterizes the First

Consonant Shift—results in still another modification of the consonantism in Proto-Germanic (see Frame 3). Notice especially that Fourquet posits an intermediate order of voiced spirants. Notice, too, that the correlations are now those of sonority uniting the *spirants*, and release or plosion uniting the *voiceless stops and spirants* of the same class (labial, dental, velar, labio-velar).

This, then, is M. Fourquet's phonological explanation of the Germanic Consonant Shift. Because of a weakening in the habits of articulation—which he admittedly postulates on the basis of an inspection and interpretation of the sound-changes involved—there took place a "chain reaction" which restructured the consonantal system of certain Indo-European dialects, among them Germanic. By positing certain intermediate stages compatible with these presumed phonetic tendencies, Fourquet establishes a direct line to the consonantism of Germanic as revealed, albeit imperfectly, in later historical records.

Incidentally, any similarity between Fourquet's explanation of the cause of the Germanic sound shifts and the notion advanced by such scholars as Heinrich Meyer-Benfey, Hermann Osthoff, and Hermann Collitz that the mutations were in large part effected by an increase in the force of expiration brought about by life in mountainous areas is only superficial and probably quite fortuitous. Fourquet attempts a phonetic interpretation of a phonology based either upon historical or reconstructed evidence; the Germans were searching for some extra-linguistic factor which might have influenced habits of articulation.

The most obvious difference between Fourquet's theory and the neogrammarian approach is that it tries to provide insight into the probable causes of the shift. This causal factor—phonetically expressed—is a change in the manner of articulation; and it is *this* change that precipitated the restructuring of the phonological system. Fourquet, in fact, reserves the term "mutation" to describe the cause rather than the results of phonetic change: ". . . a consonantal mutation is a general change in the manner of articulation, affecting a regular consonantal system, and leading to a new and [likewise] regular system" (*Les mutations consonantiques du germanique*, p. 4).

But there are other differences between the two approaches. For instance, the neogrammarians cannot determine whether in Primitive Germanic the Indo-European voiced aspirated stops (*bh, dh, gh, gʷh*) had become voiced spirants (*β, ð, γ, γʷ*), voiced unaspirated stops (*b, d, g, gʷ*), or a combination of the two in some sort of allophonic relationship to one another. Furthermore, although most Germanists posit a series of voiced spirants for Proto-Germanic—which derive in turn from the aspirated voiced stops of Pre-Germanic—there are still those scholars who prefer to set up a series of voiced stops for the Germanic proto-stage. The neogrammarian method cannot solve this problem because its reconstructions are based upon orthographic symbols which admit of two interpretations: they may be read now as stops and now as spirants. To mention just a few of the more flagrant instances: In Old Norse and Old English, the letter *f* is used for both [f] and [β], and þ and ð are used indiscriminately for both the voiceless and voiced spirants. The same is true of Old Saxon: *th* in the word *brōthar* has the sound [ð]; in other instances it stands for the voiceless spirant.

Diachronic phonology offers a solution. The Germanic mutation was triggered by a weakening of articulation, which in turn brought about a lenition that eventually affected almost the entire consonantism. The changes occasioned by this weakening of articulation are assumed to have been unconditioned, so that we must accept an intermediate stage during which the voiced aspirates became voiced spirants *in all positions*. Does this violate any direct, historical evidence we possess? Apparently not, says Fourquet, pointing to another Indo-European language—Armenian—that underwent a series of phonological changes almost identical to the ones he ascribes to the Germanic mutation. One can of course object to a procedure that is determined by a theory rather than by reconstructable evidence, but one can scarcely deny the possibility or even the reasonableness of such an intermediate stage; especially when neither the neogrammarian method nor phonemic studies based upon distribution patterns are able to provide us with information to the contrary.

Fourquet assumes voiced spirants for Proto-Germanic because this would be in full harmony with the phonological progression which he posits. This same assumption considers these sounds to have been spirants in all positions. In Primitive Germanic, on the other hand, the voiced spirants—consistent with the consequences of weakened articulation—often became stops (see Fig. 2, Frame 4). Here, however, one must reckon with a conditioning factor. Caught in a flow of air, however weak—and surrounded by sonants —these consonants would tend to be preserved as spirants. In all other environments they would become stops, and the phonetic "drift" would be toward occlusion in *all* positions. Frame 4 schematizes the possibility of the two correlations, bringing together either the spirants or the stops, as the case may be. Trying to determine the precise phonetic value of the orthographic symbols used to record this vacillating condition as it prevailed in the various Germanic dialects in historical times is of course a legitimate undertaking, but from a phonological viewpoint there is really no problem.

Diachronic structuralists point out that not only does Professor Fourquet's theory provide reasonable answers to the most knotty problems of the Germanic Consonant Shift, but when we study his structuring of the shift into correlation-bundles, we see the whole principle of mutation emerging in a more meaningful manner. The important thing is not that *sounds* change, but that *habits of articulation* change, and this in turn restructures the *sound system* of a language.

As a sort of postscript, it is interesting to take the table of the Germanic Shift as given on page 77, recast Fourquet's Pre-Germanic stage (Fig. 2, Frame 2) in linear arrangement, and let it serve as an intermediate stage between Indo-European and Germanic. Since the spirantization of the IE voiced aspirated stops—the midway point in their progression to voiced unaspirated stops—is posited for Proto-Germanic rather than for Pre-Germanic, this particular series is taken from Frame 3. Try to think in phonetic terms as you examine the chart, remembering that h indicates aspiration, and the inferior dot stands for lenition:

Indo-European	Intermediate	Germanic
p, t, k, k^w	ph, th, kh, k^{w}h	f, þ, χ, χ^w
bh, dh, gh, g^{w}h	β, ð, γ, γ^w	b, d, g, g^w (Gothic)
b, d, g, g^w	ḅ, ḍ, g, g^w	p, t, k. k^w

The similarities between Jean Fourquet's explanation of the causes of the Germanic Consonant Shift and that put forward by Jacob Grimm must surely have impressed the reader. Professor Fourquet, of course, is fully aware of Grimm's contribution, and he devotes an entire chapter to a critique of it. Because of Grimm's naïveté in things phonetic, and because he couched many of his hypotheses in romantic, even quasi-mystical language, his successors tended to play down certain phases of his work. In the decades following his death, linguistic research became increasingly positivistic and less inclined to entertain theories for which there was no factual confirmation. As a reaction to the uncontrolled and often unfounded speculations of an earlier era such conservatism and caution was understandable, but it eventually led to a kind of sterile orthodoxy that looked askance at any historical procedure venturing beyond a mere description of two successive synchronic situations, so that many linguists have long considered Grimm's Law simply a neat *description* of certain sound-changes that characterized the transition of Germanic from Primitive Indo-European. In the light of this discussion of what is meant by a structural explanation of these phenomena, I trust that the reader has by now been convinced that Grimm's real contribution was not merely a description of *what* happened (which others had seen as clearly as he), but an explanation of *how* it had happened—not in psychological terms but in *structural* terms. His language lacks precision and he was guilty of gross inconsistencies, but his intent is clear. He was far, far ahead of his time. He was, in fact, one of the first structuralists.

Saussure's teachings influenced still another scholar who was himself destined to make some original and significant contributions to linguistic theory: Louis Hjelmslev (1899——), Professor of Linguistics at the University of Copenhagen and guiding genius of the so-called "Copenhagen School." The most definitive formulation of his theories is set forth in the book *Omkring Sprogteoriens Grundlæggelse* (1943), translated into English by Francis J. Whitfield under the title *Prolegomena to a Theory of Language* (1953). Actually, most of Hjelmslev's views have been in print even longer, to be found for instance in his *Principes de grammaire générale* of 1928. The *Prolegomena*, however, constitute a rigorous and refined exposition of that system of theory and analysis to which its author has given the name "glossematics," a controversial but important contribution to modern structural linguistics. An adequate description of this highly abstract approach to language would be quite beyond the scope of this treatise, so we must content ourselves with a brief discussion of a few of its more obvious tenets. All quotations are from the English edition. Parenthetically, may I herewith acknowledge my indebtedness to Paul L. Garvin's detailed review of this work in *Language*, XXX, 1 (January–March, 1954).

Two of Saussure's theses are especially basic to glossematics: (1) that a language is a system of values; and (2) that language (*la langue*) is a form and not a substance. The key to an analysis of this form is an "immanent" linguistics that is operationally self-sufficient and self-contained, having no reference to metaphysical reality (meaning). The subject matter of this sort of linguistic analysis—the "text" or corpus being analyzed or constructed—will therefore have an existence only in terms of the patterns arrived at by these completely formal, inherently determined procedures. Glossematics thus becomes the triumph of pure form.

Hjelmslev himself summarizes the essence of the glossematic approach in these words:

> [The linguist] discovers certain properties present in all those objects that people agree to call languages, in order then to generalize those properties and establish them by

definition. From that moment the linguistic theoretician has—arbitrarily, but appropriately—himself decreed to which objects his theory can and cannot be applied. He then sets up, for all objects of the nature premised in the definition, a general calculus, in which all conceivable cases are foreseen. This calculus, which is deduced from the established definition independently of all experience, provides the tools for describing or comprehending a given text and the language on which it is constructed. Linguistic theory cannot be verified (confirmed or invalidated) by reference to such existing texts and languages. It can be controlled only by tests to show whether the calculation is self-consistent and exhaustive [p. 10].

This "immanent" linguistics is by definition a system of language-analysis that is independent of all non-linguistic phenomena, being in no way reliant upon physical, physiological, psychological, or sociological data, "a self-sufficient totality, a structure *sui generis*" (p. 2).

If this sounds like "straining at a gnat" to the uninitiated reader, let him bear in mind that the principal theoretical consideration of structural linguistics has been to find some method of reaching the realities of language. Humboldt has defined language as a *function;* Saussure sought to recognize and describe this function in terms of a *system*, but his method of establishing the system employs procedures that rely upon extra-linguistic information (psychology, for example). Hjelmslev has attempted to construct a theory of language which also recognizes that language is a system, but he has tried to find some means of verifying both the existence and the nature of this system that does not depend upon non-linguistic information for its validity. This system he derives by a series of logically verifiable propositions or theories, which, when applied to a mass of material (human discourse), yield a "text." This text, therefore, owes its existence *as text* to the operational procedures by which and according to which it was derived; its "reality" is guaranteed by the logical "reality" of the derivational procedures, and not because it had an earlier existence as undifferentiated discourse. Thus, Hjelmslev's "text" is essentially a series of deductions abstracted from the *content* (discourse), and expressed in propositions that can be subjected to the controls of *formal logic*.

The theories from which the premises are derived must all conform to the basic requirements imposed upon any theory that is to be used empirically: they must exhibit self-sufficiency, exhaustiveness, and simplicity. A theory which conforms to these three criteria can presumably be safely applied to the analysis of empirical data (experiential information or knowledge). Such a theory, however, in order to be *logically* useful must also meet the test of "arbitrariness," that is, its corollaries must follow from its premises. If they did not, then there would be no way of controlling and evaluating the results obtained by extending a theory to a given situation. But even if *logically* sound, a theory may still be "useless" in a practical sense. Any good mathematician can construct an algebra or calculus that is consistent, exhaustive, simple, and arbitrary—and quite useless, because it cannot be applied to the type of relationships presented by the empirical data. Therefore, to be useful a theory must also be *appropriate*. Hjelmslev defines a theory as "appropriate" when its premises "satisfy the conditions for application to a large number of experimental data" (p. 8).

Although its practitioners are constantly working at methods of applying it to the practical analysis of language, glossematics—as is evident from the foregoing discussion—has been chiefly concerned with theory. Ultimately, of course, its theories must prove to be "appropriate," else they become mere exercises in mental gymnastics. Actually, as of this writing, there are very few published accounts of the application of glossematic theory to the analysis of a language. Probably the most extensive is Knud Togeby's *Structure immanente de la langue française* (Copenhagen, 1951). Much less pretentious but considerably more accessible is Emilio Alarcos Llorach's *Gramática estructural* (see the Bibliography for details).

The most serious and most often expressed reservation about the value of glossematics is: "But to what extent does a Hjelmslevian analysis describe a natural language?" A glossematic exposition of a text is logically flawless; thin in inherent in the method, since the textual analysis proceeds from corollaries logically derived from the premises that determined which portions of the discourse (speech or writing) would constitute the text. But commendable as a consistently logical analysis may be, one would also appreciate some assurance that it is likewise a *linguistic* analysis.

In order to weigh this criticism, we must deal with two more terms of prime importance to glossematic theory: "expression" and "content." Hjelmslev conceives of language as consisting of these two planes, joined by the relation called a linguistic sign (Saussure!). Each plane in turn is subject to a further dichotomy in terms of *form* and *substance*. The substance of expression is "raw" phonetics; the form, on the other hand, consists of the various structural patternings of the substance—phonemes, morphemes, and so forth. Applying these same criteria to content, Hjelmslev defines the substance as the extra-linguistic part of language: the world of words and meanings. The form of content he identifies with the meaning-*structures* of a language, crudely analogous to the linguistic "fields" in the Whorfian and neo-Humboldtian sense.

To the extent that an analysis of the substance of Hjelmslevian expression (raw text) results in a complete statement of its form, glossematics will yield an operationally valid description of the data. However, if the text has in any way been restricted, that is, if the formal analysis has been limited by certain logical premises to include something less than the total structure, then to that extent the glossematic description would be incomplete and, perhaps, distorted. So much is certain. On the basis of those applications of Hjelmslev's theories that have become generally available, one may well reiterate Murray Fowler's words in his perceptive review of Knud Togeby's book: "It is at least doubtful whether the theories of glossematics . . . can be substantiated in the inspection of any one language without distorting the ultimate appearance of that language" (*Language*, XXIX, 174).

The story of the rise of structural linguistics in America has been told so often and so well, that it would be presumptuous to tell it again—at least in this book. The names of Franz Boas (1858–1942), Edward Sapir (1884–1939), and Leonard Bloomfield (1887–1948), are now familiar to anyone even superficially interested in American linguistics. Most important, of course, the ideas nurtured and developed by these pioneers have grown in this generation into a mature and vigorous system for investigating language. Textbooks like Henry A. Gleason's *An Introduction to Descriptive Linguistics*, Archibald A. Hill's *Introduction to Linguistic Structures*, and Charles F. Hockett's *A Course in Modern Linguistics*, all bear witness to the flowering of American linguistic scholarship; and all of them recognize as their spiritual progenitor Leonard Bloomfield's classic work, *Language* (New York: Henry Holt & Co., 1933). Furthermore, the principles and methods of American structuralism have by now been incorporated—to a greater or lesser extent—into many of our language texts, notably those of English. One thinks immediately of the works of Charles C. Fries, or of one of the more recent books like W. Nelson Francis' *The Structure of American English*. For those who are interested in anthologies, there are at present (1962) two excellent ones: *Applied English Linguistics*, under the editorship of Harold B. Allen, and *Readings in Linguistics*, edited by Martin Joos (the latter more concerned with theory). These—plus the vast backlog of material contained in *Language*, the publication of the Linguistic Society of America—provide a full and many-sided account of the development of American structural linguistics.

In these pages, therefore, I limit myself primarily to a discussion of certain of the ideas either formulated or championed by probably the most influential figure in American linguistics during the first half of the twentieth century: Leonard Bloomfield.

Even a provisional evaluation of Bloomfield's enormous contribution to linguistic science is not easy. In the case of Saussure and Trubetzkoy, for example, we may properly speak of a "school," for each of them established certain premises and methods that formed the foundation upon which a body of doctrine was erected. But Bloomfield did not found a "school"; indeed, he abhorred and rejected the very notion of a doctrinaire approach to language, counting in one of the signal contributions of the Linguistic Society of America that it had preserved linguistics in this country from the "blight of the odium theologicum and the postulation of 'schools.'" Nor did he train any sizable number of students in descriptive linguistics. Both Franz Boas and his student Edward Sapir were more influential as teachers. Bloomfield did make some abiding contributions to basic linguistic theory, but here again it would not be accurate to think of him as the sole fountainhead and oracle of descriptivist theory. As for pioneering the techniques of descriptive analysis, again Professors Boas and Sapir must be conceded a place of greater historical prominence. Wherein, then, does his profound and enduring influence lie?

The most satisfactory answer is probably that given by Bernard Bloch in his memorialization of Bloomfield in the journal *Language:* "There can be no doubt that Bloomfield's greatest contribution to the study of language was to make a science of it" (XXV, 92). This is an accurate judgment. Let us attempt to lend it some historical perspective.

Any discussion of Bloomfield's role in the development of linguistics must include the observation that he was by background and training a historico-comparative linguist, teaching courses in Germanic philology throughout his professorial career. Without this perspective it is impossible to appreciate his unique contribution to American scholarship, for the line from Jacob Grimm to the neogrammarians and to Bloomfield is direct and unbroken. In the sets of phonetic correspondences we refer to collectively as Grimm's Law, Bloomfield perceived that which is of fundamental importance, namely, that the sound-*patterns* of language change systematically, and that these patterns are discoverable by following certain procedures. In the *American Journal of Philology* of 1922 he wrote: "It was Grimm's merit . . . that by the strength of a method, he conquered for science a body of facts so vast that the

generations since have worked well within the bounds he reached
and scarcely ever gone beyond" (p. 373).

To Bloomfield the principle of the regularity of sound-change
was the cornerstone of linguistic science. He championed the neogrammarian position vigorously and without compromise, rebuk-
ing all those who would admit the possibility of "exceptions" to the
rule. His own wording eloquently points out how those who would
admit such irregularities are in truth denying scientific validity to
their results:

> The real point at issue is the scope of the phonetic cor-
> respondence-classes and the significance of the residues.
> The neo-grammarians claimed that the results of study
> justified us in making the correspondence-classes non-con-
> tradictory and in seeking a complete analysis of the
> residues. . . . The neo-grammarian insists, particularly,
> that his hypothesis is fruitful in this last direction: it sorts
> out the resemblances that are due to factors other than
> phonetic change, and accordingly leads us to an under-
> standing of these factors.
>
> The actual dispute, then, concerns the weeding-out of
> false etymologies, the revision of our statements of
> phonetic correspondence, and the recognition of linguistic
> changes other than sound-change.
>
> The opponents of the neo-grammarian hypothesis claim
> that resemblances which do not fit into recognized types
> of phonetic correspondence may be due merely to sporadic
> occurrence or deviation or non-occurrence of sound-
> change. Now, the very foundation of modern historical
> linguistics consisted in the setting up of phonetic cor-
> respondence-classes: in this way alone did Rask and
> Grimm bring order into the chaos of resemblances which
> had bewildered all earlier students. The advocates of
> sporadic sound-change, accordingly, agree with the neo-
> grammarians in discarding such etymologies as Latin *dies;*

English *day*, and retain only a few, where the resemblance is striking, such as Latin *habēre:* Old High German *habēn*. . . . They admit that this leaves us no criterion of decision, but insist that our inability to draw a line does not prove anything: exceptional sound-changes occurred, even though we have no certain way of recognizing them.

The neo-grammarian sees in this a serious violation of scientific method. The beginning of our science was made by a procedure which implied regularity of phonetic change, and further advances . . . were based on the same implicit assumption. It may be, of course, that some other assumption would lead to an even better correlation of facts, but the advocates of sporadic sound-change offer nothing of the kind; they accept the results of the actual method and yet claim to explain some facts by a contradictory method (or lack of method) which was tried and found wanting through all the centuries that preceded Rask and Grimm [*Language*, pp. 354–55].

Bloomfield improved upon Grimm and the neogrammarians in one highly important way: he restated their findings in "physical terms"—that is, in the language of scientific description. He eschewed figurative, metaphysical expressions, always searching instead for the everyday words of the physical world. Read, for example, his rephrasing of the neogrammarian postulate:

In the 1870's, when technical terms were less precise than today, the assumption of uniform sound-change received the obscure and metaphorical wording, "Phonetic laws have no exceptions." It is evident that the term "law" has here no precise meaning, for a sound-change is not in any sense a law, but only a historical occurrence. The phrase "have no exceptions" is a very inexact way of saying that non-phonetic factors, such as the frequency or meaning of particular linguistic forms, do not interfere with the change of phonemes [*Language*, p. 354].

This constant effort to restrict himself to "speech-forms of maximum response-uniformity" gives to his writing a certain superficial simplicity. One is tempted to skim along because his prose reads so easily. Very soon, however, the reader discovers that he must slow down and take in every word with great care, for Bloomfield writes with a precision that demands one's full attention.

Certainly one reason why his book *Language* has become a classic is that later writers have only seldom succeeded in improving upon its exposition. This does not mean that linguistics has not advanced beyond Bloomfield—of course it has—but the *facts* of language are the same now as they were then, and to the extent that those facts were known to Bloomfield, his presentation remains unexcelled. *His book continues to be the source of his greatest influence.* And rightly so. Read his explanation of what we mean when we say that languages are "related." It is difficult to imagine how one could improve by so much as a word upon the neatness and simple, almost homely directness of his style:

> When we say . . . that a resemblance between languages is due to a *relationship*, we mean that these languages are later forms of a single earlier language. In the case of the Romance languages, we have written records of this parent language, namely, Latin. After the Latin language had spread over a large area, it underwent different linguistic changes in different parts of this area, so that today these different parts differ greatly in speech, and we call the divergent speech-forms "Italian," "French," "Spanish," and so on. If we could follow the speech, say of Italy, through the last two-thousand years, we could not pick out any hour or year or century when "Latin" gave way to "Italian"; these names are entirely arbitrary. By and large, any feature that is common to all the modern territorial forms of Latin, was present in the Latin of two-thousand years ago; on the other hand, when the modern forms of Latin disagree as to any feature, then some or all of them have, in this feature, undergone

some change during the last two-thousand years. The resemblances appear especially in features that are common in everyday speech in the commonest constructions and form-classes and in the intimate basic vocabulary. The features of difference, moreover, appear in systematic groups, with each territorial form diverging in its own characteristic way [*Language*, p. 298].

One cannot paraphrase language of such succinctness and clarity; one can only quote it.

In his study of Saussure's *Cours*, Bloomfield came to appreciate keenly the distinction the Swiss scholar had set up between *parole* and *langue*. In the latter he recognized a body of information amenable to scientific investigation, for *la langue* is by definition a supra-individualistic system abstracted from the flow of living speech, incorporating only those features common to all speakers of a community, and resulting in an impersonal and rigid complex that can be subjected to controlled investigation. Of critical theoretical significance to Bloomfield, moreover, was that this system is not simply the sum of all the speech acts of a community, but rather that *la langue* is a system of *patterns* which by virtue of their *contrastive features* function as linguistic signals. Saussurian theory, therefore, forms the basis of much of Bloomfield's own thinking about descriptive or structural linguistics.

He was of course thoroughly conversant with the descriptivist techniques pioneered by the two American anthropologists, Franz Boas and Edward Sapir. As early as 1917 he published his *Tagalog Texts with Grammatical Analysis*, using essentially the now familiar procedures for determining the phonemic and morphemic patterns of a language. He saw in these procedures not only a scientifically acceptable method of language analysis, but also a logical and categorical extension of the basic premises of historical linguistics. Not *sound*-change but systematic change of sound-*patterns* was the great discovery of Jacob Grimm. And to this the neogrammarians had added the principle of *regularity*. These changes were beyond the control of the individual speaker, constituting in their entirety the abstract system of sounds contained in that supra-individual-istic language which Saussure had named *la langue*. Structural linguistics, therefore, was nothing but a technique for progressing from *sounds* to sound-*patterns*, from *parole* to *langue*. In Bloom-field's approach to this principle of patterning, however, we have perhaps his greatest contribution to linguistic theory.

Saussure had used patterning to account for changes in value; the Prague linguists developed it into a method for studying the functional interrelationships of the *sounds* of a language. Specifical-ly, they were interested in structuralism as a technique for demon-strating the interrelationship of form and meaning. Language, said Saussure, is a system of signs, a joining of the signifier and the signified, of form and meaning. How does one determine which meaning goes with which form? The Prague researchers supplied their own answer: by substituting phonetic segments in identical environments, in order to determine whether such substitutions bring about a change of meaning. Meaning, therefore, becomes the ultimate criterion of identification. Or, to put it differently, the operational procedure for isolating and defining the phoneme is based upon a *functional* equivalence; and this discriminative func-tion of the phoneme, in turn, is based upon a *semantic* assumption.

Precisely at this point Bloomfield broke with his European col-leagues. He rejected in principle a system of language analysis that was dependent upon non-linguistic criteria for its results. *Meaning, insisted Bloomfield, must be investigated through formal (structural) differences in a language, since it is just these formal differences that determine differences in meaning.*

This mechanistic approach to structure carries with it a revised definition of the phoneme, for from this point of view it can no longer be considered a semantic concept; nor can it be defined as a physical or acoustic entity, since it can be neither observed directly nor measured by instruments. Bloomfield would therefore define the phoneme as a *feature of language structure;* the phonemes of a lan-guage become a set of abstractions for describing certain features of the utterances of a language.

Bloomfield's insistence that non-linguistic criteria must not enter into a grammatical description of a language brought the charge so frequently and monotonously leveled against him that he proposed to analyze language without reference to meaning. In answering this charge, let us first hear what Bloomfield himself has to say about meaning:

> The study of speech-sounds without regard to meanings is an abstraction: in actual use, speech-sounds are uttered as signals. We have defined the *meaning* of a linguistic form as the situation in which the speaker utters it and the response which it calls forth in the hearer. . . . The situations which prompt people to utter speech, include every object and happening in their universe. In order to give a scientifically accurate definition of meaning for every form of a language, we should have to have a scientifically accurate knowledge of everything in the speaker's world. The actual extent of human knowledge is very small, compared to this. . . . We can define the names of minerals, for example, in terms of chemistry and mineralogy . . . , but we have no precise way of defining words like *love* or *hate*. . . . The statement of meanings is therefore the weak point in language-study, and will remain so until human knowledge advances very far beyond its present state. In practice, we define the meaning of a linguistic form, wherever we can, in terms of some other science. Where this is impossible, we resort to makeshift devices. One is *demonstration*. . . . This is essentially the process by which children learn the use of speech-forms. If a questioner understood enough of our language, we could define the word . . . for him by *circumlocution*— that is, in the manner of our dictionaries. . . . Or else, if we knew enough of the questioner's language, we could answer him by *translation* [*Language*, pp. 139–40].

The above, I submit, contains nothing heretical or intellectually repugnant. It is merely a statement of fact: we cannot define words very well. Mathematicians and logicians have had to invent their own languages based upon a self-contained calculus, the meaning of which can be controlled by built-in principles. When dealing with the phenomena of the world about them, linguists have no special way of getting at meaning: they use the makeshift devices to which Bloomfield alludes, such as demonstration and circumlocution. But when speaking about language itself, they have tried to develop a scientific method of description which avoids definitions in terms of mind. And it is probably because of this that some people maintain that the "Bloomfieldians" deny the importance of meaning in language study. It is true that Bloomfield rejected in principle a system of language analysis that is dependent upon non-linguistic criteria for its results. *Grammatical* meaning, he insisted, must be determined by reference to the formal (structural) differences in a language, since it is just these formal contrasts that determine the differences in linguistic meaning.

One thinks immediately of the parts of speech as defined by the traditional grammarians. "A noun is the name of a person, place, or thing" is palpably useless as a definition, since it contains no grammatical information. Provided we had accurate criteria for determining which items in our environment are persons, places, and things, we could conceivably compile a list of words and agree to refer to them as "nouns." But we would still not have the slightest hint as to how these "nouns" fitted into the linguistic system we call "language." This critical information can only be learned by noting the structural features that differentiate these forms from other forms. Eventually, of course, we discover the specific criteria which permit us to group together certain morphemes in the language into form-classes. At this point the linguist can formulate a physical definition of a "noun" in terms of structural and distributional patterns. The scientific validity of our definition is confirmed when a native speaker responds in a predictable way to the patterns we have established.

Bloomfield was vitally interested in meaning, but he strove for physical definitions that were scientifically verifiable and controllable. He states his case quite simply: "The mentalists would supplement the facts of language by a version in terms of mind. . . . The mechanists demand that the facts be presented without any assumption of such auxiliary factors" (*Language*, p. vii).

In summary I should like to quote the words of Bernard Bloch, Professor of Linguistics at Yale University, long-time editor of *Language*, and a colleague of Bloomfield:

> It is not too much to say that every significant refinement of analytic method produced in this country since 1933 has come as a direct result of the impetus given to linguistic research by Bloomfield's book. If today our methods are in some ways better than his, if we see more clearly than he did himself certain aspects of structure that he first revealed to us, it is because we stand upon his shoulders [*Language*, XXV, 92].

To the extent that it was given over to a clarification and elaboration of the theories and methods set forth in Bloomfield's *Language*, the period from 1933 to about 1950 may appropriately be called the "Bloomfieldian era" in the history of American linguistic scholarship. We shall end our discussion of perspectives in linguistics by mentioning a very few of the highlights of this era.

Although the influence of his text was far-reaching and profound, it should be noted that Bloomfield actually wrote little about specific procedures and techniques. The task of elaborating suitable methods, therefore, was in the main left to those scholars who sought to adapt his approach to the operational requirements of the practical linguist—often the anthropologist or the missionary. Here the names of Kenneth L. Pike and Eugene A. Nida must be singled out.

Professor Pike contributed two key volumes to the burgeoning science of descriptive linguistics: his *Phonetics* of 1942 and his *Phonemics* of 1947 (available in mimeographed form in 1943). An outstanding feature of the *Phonetics* was that it included precise descriptions couched in articulatory terminology of many speech-sounds that until then had in general escaped the attention of phoneticians because they did not occur in the better-known Western European languages. Pike's interest, however, centered on the aboriginal languages of the Western hemisphere. Such information was sorely needed, for the American structuralists of that time were especially concerned with describing these indigenous languages of the Americas. He also stressed the importance of *environment* as a factor influencing the pronunciation of a given sound. This, too, had been slighted by phoneticians of the traditional stripe.

His *Phonemics* was for years the most widely used handbook of its kind (and, for that matter, may still be). Highly practical, with step-by-step directions for doing the exercises, the chief value of this richly informative guide "for reducing languages to writing" stemmed from its author's intimate knowledge of the many languages and dialects of the Americas. Both volumes were used as training manuals (as was Nida's *Morphology*) in the Summer Institute of Linguistics, of which Dr. Pike has long been director.

A practical handbook of morphemic analysis was provided by Eugene A. Nida, executive secretary of the American Bible Society and also long active in the Summer Institute of Linguistics. His *Morphology: The Descriptive Analysis of Words* first appeared in 1946, undergoing an extensive revision in 1949, at which time its value was substantially enhanced by the inclusion of copious examples from the Indian languages of Mexico. For wealth of illustrative material and detailed instructions for field procedures, Nida's *Morphology* is still unexcelled.

The thirties and forties also witnessed the painstaking and arduous labors of American structuralists to clarify and secure the theoretical basis of their science. Over these years the pages of the journal of the Linguistic Society of America, *Language*, contained article after article from the pens of such outstanding theoreticians as Bernard Bloch, Zellig S. Harris, Charles F. Hockett, Henry Lee Smith, Jr., Morris Swadesh, and George L. Trager, to mention only a few of the more active scholars. Problems relating to the nature and function of the phoneme were among the first to be studied. Typical were the articles devoted to phonemic overlapping, juncture, the identification and classification of allophones, and the phonemics of English syllabics. Although the ultimate answer to these and other questions is in some cases still to come, research in this area had progressed far enough to warrant the publication in 1948 of Bernard Bloch's now classic article, "A Set of Postulates for Phonemic Analysis" (*Language*, XXIV, 3–46).

Once the analytical methods for a phonemic structuralization of language had been derived, scholars began shifting their attention to the higher levels of morphology and syntax. Although the achievements here were not as unambiguous as in the area of phonemics, no less effort was expended. Characteristic of this type of research were the many studies devoted to a morphemic analysis of form classes, the more general problem of morpheme identification and segmentation, and attempts to define the *word*. Syntax—where it seemed profitable to discuss it separately—proved less amenable to the analytical methods of early structural linguistics, although there are several excellent studies dating from those years, such as Charles F. Hockett's "Potawatomi Syntax" (*Language*, XV, 1939).

At the far end of what we have chosen to call the "Bloomfieldian era" stands a most rigorous and book-length attempt to organize all of American structuralism into a single body of theory and practice: Zellig S. Harris' *Methods in Structural Linguistics* (1951). In this formidable work Harris attempted to establish a set of structural methods which could describe a language completely in terms of "the logic of distributional relations." With the publication of *Methods in Structural Linguistics* American structuralism clearly reached its majority, and could take its place in the world of scholarship as a mature discipline uncompromisingly dedicated to the scientific study of language.

TABLE 1

PHONETIC SYMBOLS

(Selected to illustrate examples occurring in the text)

	Bilabials		Labio-Dentals		Dentals		Palatals		Velars	
Stops	p	b			t	d	č	ǰ	k	g
Spirants	ɸ	β	f	v	θ	ð	š	ž	χ	γ
					s	z				
Nasals		m				n		ñ		ŋ
Laterals						l		ll		L
Trills						r				R

1. Each series is divided into "voiceless" and "voiced."
2. Under "Dental Spirants" are grouped both the slit and grooved variety.

TABLE 2

VOWELS

	Front	Central	Back
High	i		u
Lower-high	ɪ		ʊ
Higher-mid	e		o
Mean-mid		ə	
Lower-mid	ɛ		ɔ
Higher-low	æ		
Low		a	

Additional symbols:

    1. Lenition—a dot placed beneath a symbol: [ḅ].

    2. Aspiration—' placed at the upper right of a symbol: [p'].

    3. Vowel length—in phonetic transcription a colon [e:]; in conventional orthography the macron: *frāter*.

    4. Lengthening of the dental trill—a macron placed over the syllable: [r̄] as in Spanish *perro*.

    5. Syllabicity—a small circle placed beneath a symbol: [m̥].

    6. Primary stress—' placed above the vowel of the syllable bearing primary stress: English *agó*.

SELECTED BIBLIOGRAPHY

The Older Periods

GRAY, LOUIS. *Foundations of Language.* New York, 1939. Probably the most detailed and complete study in English. Traditional in its approach. Presupposes good background in languages. Excellent bibliography.

JESPERSEN, OTTO. *Language, Its Nature, Development and Oriyin.* New York, 1922. In many ways the most satisfactory book of its kind. Clearly and simply written, it presupposes only an intelligent interest in language.

PEDERSEN, HOLGER. *Linguistic Science in the Nineteenth Century.* Translated by John Spargo. Cambridge, 1931. A detailed and scholarly account of linguistic history from its beginnings, with special emphasis on the development of Indo-European comparative linguistics. Many photographs, illustrations, and specimen texts.

WHITNEY, WILLIAM DWIGHT. *Language and the Study of Language.* New York, 1874. Primarily of historical interest. Nevertheless, these printed lectures by the first internationally known American linguist are still richly informative and highly readable.

The Modern Period

BLOOMFIELD, LEONARD. *Language.* New York, 1933. The best general introduction to the scientific study of language. Must be read carefully. Excellent bibliography.

CARROLL, JOHN B. *The Study of Language.* Cambridge, Mass., 1955. A history of language study in America, both as an independent discipline and as it relates to other research areas. Good bibliography.

GLEASON, HENRY A. *An Introduction to Descriptive Linguistics.* New York, 1955. 2d rev. ed., 1961. Excellent introduction to American structuralism. Clearly and accurately written with emphasis on basic principles and methods. *Workbook* published separately.

HALL, ROBERT A. "American Linguistics, 1925–50," *Archivum Linguisticum,* Vol. III, fasc. 2; Vol. IV, fasc. 1. Primarily useful for its detailed bibliographical references.

———. *Leave Your Language Alone!* Ithaca, N.Y., 1950. 2d rev. ed.; *Linguistics and Your Language,* New York, 1960. A somewhat tendentious but interesting and lively discussion of language from the viewpoint of the modern American structuralist. Intended for the beginner.

HJELMSLEV, LOUIS. *Prolegomena to a Theory of Language.* Translated by Francis J. Whitfield. Baltimore, 1953. The authoritative handbook of glossematic theory. Should only be attempted by the advanced student, and even then only after adequate orientation.

HUGHES, JOHN P. *The Science of Language.* New York, 1962. A well-written and clear account of the history, theories, and methods of the scientific study of language. Highly recommended for the beginner. Very useful bibliography.

LLORACH, EMILIO ALARCOS. *Fonología española según el método de la Escuela de Praga.* 2d ed. Madrid, 1954. The best introduction to the theories and methods of Prague structuralism of which I am aware. Simple style and clear presentation. There is nothing comparable in English.

———. *Gramática estructural según la Escuela de Copenhague y con especial atención a la lengúa español.* Madrid, 1951. Not as successful in its objective as the previous item. Listed here because it is one of the few published attempts to apply glossematic theory with an aim toward clarification.

MOHRMANN, CHRISTINE, SOMMERFELT, ALF, AND WHATMOUGH, JOSHUA (eds.). *Trends in European and American Linguistics.* Antwerp, 1961. A thorough survey of recent professional activity in linguistics. Copious bibliographies.

SAPIR, EDWARD. *Language.* New York, 1921. A fascinating discussion of language as an instrument of human communication. Non-technical and highly readable.

DE SAUSSURE, FERDINAND. *Course in General Linguistics.* Translated by Wade Baskin. New York, 1959. Probably the most significant text on linguistics to be published in the twentieth century (French original, 1916). Marks the beginning of systematic structural linguistics in the Western world.

STURTEVANT, EDGAR H. *An Introduction to Linguistic Science.* New Haven: 1947. A simple, straightforward, introductory text. Interesting treatment of types of sound-change.

TRUBETZKOY, NIKOLAS S. *Grundzüge der Phonologie.* Prague, 1939. There is a French translation of this: *Principes de phonologie,* trans. J. Cantineau (Paris, 1949). This important work is the definitive exposition of Prague School structuralism, although much of Trubetzkoy's material has undergone subsequent refinement and improvement. Not easy and not recommended as an introduction to structural linguistics.

INDEX

Ablaut, 44–46
Adam, 1
Adelung, Johann Christoph, 12
Alexander de Villa Dei, 11
Alexander the Great, 8
Alexandrian Age, 8
Allen, Harold B., 87
Analogy, 51–52
Appolonios Dyskolos, 8
Aristarchus, 8
Aristotle, 6–7, 62
Ascoli, Graziadio Isaia, 43

Bally, Charles, 61
Baskin, Wade, 61
Becanus, Goropius, 13
Bible, 1; translations of, 11
Bloch, Bernard, 88, 96, 97, 98
Bloomfield, Leonard, 55, 57, 87–96
  passim
Boas, Franz, 87, 88, 92
Boghaz-köi, 44
Bopp, Franz, 30–31
Bredsdorff, Jakob Hornemann, 26
Brugmann, Karl, 42, 56
Busbecq, Ogier Ghiselin van, 12

Carbon-14 dating, 57–60
Carroll, John B., 68
Cases, names of, 7–8
Catherine the Great, 14
Chaucer, Geoffrey, 76
Christianity, influence on language
  study of, 11
Collitz, Hermann, 43, 79
Comparative method, 14, 16–19, 32–
  38, 55–57, 91–92
Consonants. See Germanic Consonant
  Shift
Constantinople, 10, 12
Copenhagen school. See Glossematics

Courtenay, J. Baudouin de, 69
Cratylus, 5–6

Darwin, Charles Robert, 31
Delbrück, Berthold, 56
Diachronic phonology (phonemics),
  77–82
Dictionaries, Indo-European, 39–40
Dionysios Thrax, 8
Donatus, Aelius, 9
Dyen, Isidore, 57

Etymology, 5–7, 10, 13, 16, 39–40

Fick, August, 39–40
Field-theory (linguistic), 67–68
Fourquet, Jean, 77–80
Fowler, Murray, 86
Francis, Nelson Winthrop, 87
Fries, Charles Carpenter, 87

Garvin, Paul L., 83
Germanic Consonant Shift, 21–30;
  structural explanation of, 77–82
Gesner, Konrad, 12
Gleason, Henry Allen, Jr., 87
Glossematics, 83–87
Glottochronology. See Lexicostatis-
  tics
Gradation. See Ablaut
Grammatical change, 25
Greeks, 5–9
Greenberg, Joseph H., 57
Grimm, Jacob, 19–30 passim, 44, 49,
  82, 88, 90, 92
Grimm's Law. See Germanic Conso-
  nant Shift
Guichard, E., 13

Harris, Zellig S., 97, 98
Hegel, Georg Wilhelm Friedrich, 31,
  35–36

Herder, Johann Gottfried von, 13, 15
Hermogenes, 6
Herodotos, 2
Hervás y Panduro, Lorenzo, 12
Hesychios, 8–9
High German Consonant Shift, 21, 26–28
Hill, Archibald A., 87
Hirt, Hermann, 56
Hittite, 34–35, 43–48
Hjelmslev, Louis, 83–86 *passim*
Hockett, Charles Francis, 87, 97, 98
Humboldt, Wilhelm von, 38, 61, 67, 86

Indians, 2–5
Indic. *See* Sanskrit

Jakobson, Roman, 68, 72
James IV (Scotland), 13
Jespersen, Otto, 75–76
Jones, Sir William, 13, 15–16, 21
Joos, Martin, 87

Karcevskij, Sergei, 72
Kemke, A., 13
Kurylowicz, Jerzy, 44, 47

Language: collections, 12; life-cycle of, 36–38; theories of origins of, 1–2, 5–7, 15; types of, 11, 35–36. *See* specific headings for additional listings
Laryngeal theory, 44–48
Lehmann, Winfred Philipp, 44, 48
Leibniz, Baron Gottfried Wilhelm von, 13–15
Leskien, August, 50, 54
Lexicostatistics, 57–60
Libby, Willard F., 58–59
Llorach, Emilio Alarcos, 85

Martinet, André, 72
Meaning, 94–96
Megiser, Hieronymus, 12
Meillet, Antoine, 56
Meyer-Benfey, H., 79
Möller, Hermann, 47

Morphology, Bopp's theory of development, 30–31
Mutation. *See* Ablaut

Neogrammarians (*Junggrammatiker*), 50, 52–55 *passim*, 79–80 *passim*, 89–90
Nida, Eugene A., 96–97

Osthoff, Hermann, 79

Pallas, P. S., 12, 14
Pāṇini, 3
Patañjali, 3
Paul, Hermann, 55
Peter the Great, 14
Philosophical grammar, 9, 12
Phoneme, 64, 69–72, 92–93
Pike, Kenneth L., 96–97
Plato, 5–7, 10
Pokorny, Julius, 40
Port Royal Grammar, 12
Porzig, Walter, 67
Pott, August, 38
Prague School, linguistic theories of, 68–76, 93
Priscian, 10
Prokosch, Eduard, 22
Psammetichos, 2, 13

Quintilian, 9

Rask, Rasmus, 18–24 *passim*, 26
Romans, 9–10

St. Isidore of Seville, 10
Sanskrit, 2–5, 16, 30–31, 36–37, 40–42
Sapir, Edward, 57, 87, 92
Saussure, Ferdinand de, 42–48 *passim*, 61–68, 72, 83, 84, 87, 93
Saussurian theory, 61–68, 87, 93
Schleicher, August, 31–43
Scholastics, 11
Sechehaye, Albert, 61
Smith, Henry Lee, Jr., 97
Socrates, 6
Sound-change, exceptions to, 50–54. *See* under specific headings for additional listings

Stoics, 7
Structuralism, American, 87–98
Swadesh, Morris, 58–60, 97
Syllabics, Indo-European, 42–43

Thomsen, Vilhelm, 43
Togeby, Knud, 85, 86
Trager, George L., 97
Trier, Jost, 67
Trivium, 11
Trubetzkoy, Prince Nikolas, 68–72
    passim, 87

Varro, 9
Vedic. *See* Sanskrit
Verner, Karl, 48, 50
Verner's Law, 48–50
Vowels: Indo-European, 41–42; shift
    in Middle English of, 75–76

Walde, Alois, 40
Weisgerber, Leo, 67
Whitfield, Francis J., 83
Whorf, Benjamin Lee, 67–68, 86

Zeno, 7